A HERALD DIARY JOKE BOOK
LAUGHTER
LINES

A HERALD DIARY JOKE BOOK

LAUGHTER LINES

A PURRFECT COMPILATION
OF PUN AND GAMES

LORNE JACKSON

BLACK & WHITE PUBLISHING

First published in the UK in 2022 by
Black & White Publishing Ltd
Nautical House, 104 Commercial Street, Edinburgh, EH6 6NF

A division of Bonnier Books UK
4th Floor, Victoria House, Bloomsbury Square, London, WC1B 4DA
Owned by Bonnier Books
Sveavägen 56, Stockholm, Sweden

Copyright © Lorne Jackson & Newsquest (Herald & Times) Ltd 2022

All rights reserved.
No part of this publication may be reproduced,
stored or transmitted in any form by any means, electronic,
mechanical, photocopying or otherwise, without the
prior written permission of the publisher.

The right of Lorne Jackson to be identified as Author of this
work has been asserted by him in accordance with the
Copyright, Designs and Patents Act, 1988.

Internal illustrations & front cover illustration (cat) © Shutterstock
Front cover illustration (wall) © Adobe Stock

A CIP catalogue record for this book is available from the British Library.

ISBN: 978 1 78530 422 4

1 3 5 7 9 10 8 6 4 2

Typeset by Black & White Publishing
Printed and bound in Great Britain by Clays Ltd, Elcograf S.p.A.

www.blackandwhitepublishing.com

CONTENTS

INTRODUCTION

The Herald newspaper is a wondrous object with many uses. For instance, with only a few years training in the sacred art of origami, you will be able to fold, crease and rip your daily *Herald* until it is transformed into a raincoat and pair of wellington boots.

There is only one minor problem connected with owning a raincoat and wellington boots made entirely out of paper.

They're liable to dissolve in the rain.

Still, no need to be unduly concerned. All you have to do is buy a second raincoat and pair of wellington boots from your local clothing boutique, which can then be worn over your origami creations, keeping them nice and dry underneath.

The Herald can also be read, of course. Many people believe this is its best use, by far. Its loyal band of readers have always delighted in their favourite paper's informative reporting of the day's events, revelling in the richness of the prose, the scholarly erudition of the journalists and the dramatic impact of the photographs.

The news can sometimes be a tad depressing however, what with all those foreign wars, corrupt politicians, superficial celebrities and potholes appearing in the roads. Occasionally there is a more upbeat tale to tell. A cat being rescued from a tree, perhaps. Though inevitably that cat will disappear down a pothole, never to be seen again.

Because the world is such a miserable place, *The Herald* long ago took the inspired decision to cheer its readers up with a daily Diary, which I have the good fortune to edit. Though, in truth, it's the readers who do most of the merrymaking, as they continuously bombard our newspaper with a barrage of bonkers jokes, a selection of which are collected in this book.

Some of the following gags are silly. Many are inspired. All will hopefully make you giggle. Jokes can also be informative, just like a good newspaper. They help explain how the world works. Or fails to work. So perhaps the following one-liners aren't merely humorous little tales. They represent the daily news cycle ... with added punchlines. Not so much *Reporting Scotland* as *Reporting Jokeland*.

And, hey, if you don't find yourself laughing uproariously by the end of this volume, you can always use your origami skills to turn the book into a spiffy helicopter, which will whisk you away for an exotic holiday (if it doesn't plummet into a pesky pothole first).

Lorne Jackson
Herald Diary Editor
(& Joke Aficionado)

1
CAVEMAN CAPERING . . .
AND BEYOND

WHAT was the very first joke, you may wonder? Most likely it didn't involve linguistic prowess, but instead was an early example of slapstick, with one angry caveman storming over to another caveman and grunting something like:

'Ugh! Wa aba-boo-ba. Grarr!'

Which translates from ancient caveman lingo into modern English as:

'I say, old chap. I noticed that you munched more than your fair share of mammoth steak at luncheon today. How terribly, terribly gauche of you.'

At which point the irate caveman bonks his former chum over the head with a hefty club.

Cue delighted chortles from a group of watching cavemen spectators, who suddenly discover that not only do they know how to make fire and forge a rudimentary wheel.

They also have a sense of humour.

The jokes in the following chapter are a lot more sophisticated than that early attempt at prehistoric drollery. In the following pages we analyse the wickedness of steps, marital stress, the angst of ageing and the athletic prowess of large, semiaquatic reptiles.

Though just in case there are a few cavemen browsing this book, we've included a rather crude gag about breaking wind.

Something for everyone, in fact.

CLAIRVOYANTLY MINDED reader Laura Price has a prediction for the future:

'Taxidermists will be replaced by Uberdermists.'

A ROMANTIC tale from Glasgow Uni student Phil Hamilton, who says:

'Me and my girlfriend have a textbook relationship. It's way too expensive.'

WE'RE NOT sure we believe reader Robin Gilmour, who assures us 'vegetarian' is an ancient Indian word that means 'bad hunter'.

WELL TRAVELLED reader Sue Neely says Hawaiian people don't laugh loudly.

'It's just a low ha,' she explains.

'I DON'T trust stairs,' says reader Sam McDaniel. 'They're always up to something.'

A RATHER daft gag that was once inflicted on us by a reader, who quite understandably refused to let us reveal his name in print:

'Why do vegetarians prefer eating rocks from earth rather than rocks from the moon? Because moon rock is a little meteor.'

A READER once mulled over the thrills of being young compared to the angst of middle age. He described it thus . . .

'Then: Long hair.

Now: Longing for hair.'

IT'S A sad truth that genius often goes unacclaimed. Reader Bruce Michaels says:

'The person who invented zero had nothing to show for it.'

AN UNLIKELY tale from reader Sheila Miller, who tells us:

'I saw someone throwing Stephen King books at people. I asked why they were doing that, then *IT* hit me.'

A FORMER serving police officer told us about a sergeant he worked with who was nicknamed 'Signal'. Apparently, he was a tube with stripes.

TEARING OPEN the Christmas crackers early this year to get his eager mitts on the daft gags inside, reader Jeremy Brown found this question to tickle us with:

'What do you call a chicken in a shell suit?' The answer is, of course . . . 'an egg'.

A CARD assistant in a Glasgow city centre shop noticed a chap who had been lingering at the anniversary cards for some time, so she finally asked if there was a problem:

'Yes,' he replied mournfully. 'I can't find one my wife will believe.'

GOVERNMENT MINISTERS claim it may be possible to spread covid through flatulence.

'My wife has declared me a national health hazard,' says reader Bob Jamieson.

IN ONE of its more educational moments, *The Herald Diary* once pointed out that if a bald chap wishes to appear as though he has a full head of hair, he always has the option of smearing Marmite on his scalp.

THIS THOUGHT reminded reader Derek Blakey of the story of the bald fellow with a rabbit balanced squarely on his head.

'Which from a distance looked like hare,' says Derek.

AN UNLIKELY tale from Arthur Kirkpatrick from Largs. Or do we mean a pair of unlikely tails?

'Two church mice came to my door,' says Arthur. 'They wanted to speak to me about cheeses.'

FINDING HERSELF continually frustrated by technology, reader Jane Roberts says:

'Autocorrect and I have a love hat relationship.'

A BRAIN teaser from reader Sonia Petersen:

'If a lady's formal dress is "evening wear" what's her knight's suit of armour called?' The answer is, of course . . . 'Silverwear'.

'**I ALWAYS** wished the sea was made of orangeade,' says a reader. 'It's my Fanta sea.'

NERVOUS READER Norman Johnstone is concerned that his stomach will resemble the pandemic once the Christmas revelries are over.

'It'll take ages to flatten the curve,' he sighs.

'**I CAN** tell when my wife drinks,' say Oliver Burton. 'Her face gets blurred.'

OUR READERS are devising New Year resolutions.

'I want to go skydiving before I die,' says Tam Smith. 'Though not RIGHT before I die.'

SPENDTHRIFT READER Edward Evans says:
  'I bought too many antiques recently. Now I'm baroque.'

'TWO PEOPLE were at my front door lecturing me on the benefits of brown bread,' says Andrew Robertson. 'They were Hovis witnesses.'

THOUGHT FOR the day from reader Beryl Young:
  'If swimming is such good exercise, why are whales always so darned chubby?'

'HOW DO you start a pudding race?' asks Mike Minton. 'Saygo.'

A RATHER disgusting story from Andy Miller, who says:

'I brought up a spaniel furball this morning. That's the last time I have a hair of the dog.'

BUZZING US on the phone, reader Phil Branson asks us:

'Where did Noah keep his bees? In archives, of course.'

WE ALL have our own way of doing things. For instance, Glasgow comedian Paul McDaniel says:

'I put milk and teabag in first.'

He adds:

'Weird way to brush your teeth, I know.'

THE SON of reader Dan Charlton is interested in astronomy and asked his dad how stars die.

'Usually from an overdose,' explained Dad.

A DEEP and profound thought from reader Edward Lowther, who says:

'A crocodile can swim faster than me, but I can run faster than a crocodile. So, in the Olympic triathlon, it would all come down to who is the better cyclist.'

SOME USEFUL advice from reader Gavin Blake, who says:

'If at first you don't succeed, try drinking beer while you're doing it. You'll be amazed at how much less you care.'

'I'VE STARTED telling everyone about the benefits of eating dried grapes,' says reader Jim Hamilton. 'It's all about raisin awareness.'

PUBLIC SPIRITED Alex Paton once got in touch with *The Herald* to enquire if any of our readers had lost a thousand pounds wrapped in elastic bands.

'I've found your elastic bands,' he added.

FANCYING A treat, reader Gordon Moir ordered a pizza for him and his wife. The food arrived, which Gordon fetched from outside his door with more excitement than usual, as there were three boxes rather than the two requested. Had the delivery folk messed up and sent an extra meal? Alas, no. One box was empty.

'That's the diet option,' said Gordon's wife.

ROD STEWART says guzzling wine helped him write his greatest hits, all of which have stood the test of time. Reader Martin Walton also produces something exceptional and long-lasting when on the vino.

'It's called a stonking great headache,' he admits.

SOME USEFUL advice from reader Lucy Thompson, who says:

'Never have a pillow fight with death unless you're willing to face the reaper cushions.'

GOURMET FRANK Morgan claims he lunched at a religious restaurant named 'The Lord Giveth'.

'They also do takeaways,' says Frank.

PLEASE TAKE your seats ladies and gentlemen. We are now proud to present the first (and possibly last) in a series of miniature plays which bravely tackle subjects of a controversial nature. Today's theatrical extravaganza, provided by reader Jim Hamilton, examines the baleful effects of having a poor parental role model. Furthermore, this hard-hitting drama doesn't shy away from shining a harsh spotlight on the greater network of societal problems, such as the wilful and malicious destruction of property. Curtain up . . .

Character One: 'Dad, are we pyromaniacs?'
Character Two: 'Yes, we arson.'

'I ALWAYS get chutney and pickle mixed up,' admits reader Jim Carver. 'It makes me chuckle.'

THERE ARE some unusual ways of advertising dairy products. Which reminds reader Richard Davis of the Christmas when his local supermarket put on a nativity scene with Babybel cheeses.

WE FIND ourselves lurking in the pub, courtesy of reader Jim Hamilton, who tells us:

'A commander walks into a bar and orders everyone around.'

'THERE'S SOMETHING I don't like about "Do Not Touch" signs,' says reader Peter Harris. 'I just can't put my finger on it.'

2
UH-OH. IT'S . . . BOJO

TRIGGER WARNING: The following chapter includes rather a lot of fearsome monsters, so you may want to read a certain number of these gags while holding the hand of a loved one, just to give you added comfort and courage.

In the next few pages, you are liable to bump into a shambling, muttering creature called 'BoJo'. There's also a hulking, sulking monstrosity going by the name of . . . 'The Donald'.

For those who prefer their scary dudes and dames

to be more commonplace and cliched, Dracula makes an appearance too.

Though he's not half as terrifying as the first couple of chaps we mentioned. Probably because at least he's only fictional (or maybe not. We'll check with the Transylvanian Tourist Board).

You should also prepare yourself for the terrors of speed dating, death by drowning, a haunting, plus a fearsome Tyrannosaurus Rex.

Don't be unduly concerned, for not all of the following tales are in the horror genre (we couldn't possibly be so cruel to our lovely readers). So, get ready for additional scoopfuls of yummy ice-cream and some exceedingly healthy vegetables . . .

SCIENTIFICALLY MINDED reader Cal Miller provides us with a handy guide to chromosomes:

XY = Male
XX = Female
YYY = Delilah

A HANDY hint from reader Tony Thompson:
    'Change your password to 'incorrect' and then if you can't quite remember it, your computer will say 'your password is incorrect'.

GLASGOW COMEDIAN Paul McDaniel has an excellent idea for a film. A meeting is held for people who suffer from Imposter Syndrome. But one person isn't supposed to be there . . .

OUR READERS are often high achievers. Jenny Clarke, for instance, has much to take pride in.

'I don't mean to boast,' she says. 'But I just finished a fourteen-day diet in one hour thirteen minutes.'

THE WIFE of reader Mark Garner hates hubby's wordplay gags and wants him to use his creative powers to write a fictional book instead. So Mark said to his wife:

'That's a novel idea.'

A TALE of violent imagery and possible redemption.

'A friend told me he hopes I die in a deep hole filled with water,' says reader William Briggs. 'Though I know he means well.'

A SCHOOLYARD yarn, where we discover that our wise educators are very astute at making logical deductions.

A fellow teacher once told Brian Logan from Langside that he was going to the Virgin Islands for his summer holidays. When Brian asked why, he replied that he had gone to the Canary Islands the year before and never saw a canary.

A STORY with added bite:

'What's worse than finding a maggot in your apple?' says Henry Muir. 'Finding half a maggot in your apple.'

A BAMBOOZLING and bonkers gag from Helen Lawson.

'How many surrealists does it take to change a lightbulb? Fish.'

ON A similar topic.

'How many divorced men does it take to change a lightbulb?' asks Terry Farmer. 'Who knows. They never get to keep the house.'

UNFORTUNATE READER Paul Beattie tells us he got in an argument with a hardcase from Glasgow's East End.

'He said he was going to mop the floor with my face,' says Paul. 'I said, "You'll be sorry. You won't be able to get in the corners very well."'

AN ELDERLY lady was sitting in her front garden in Newton Mearns when a driver stopped to ask for directions.

'How do you get into town?' he yelled.

'Usually my son takes me,' said the old lady.

'WHAT DO you give the man who has everything?' enquires William Beane. 'Antibiotics.'

A POSSIBLY apocryphal tale from reader Jim Morrison. He tells us footballer Wayne Rooney is a huge Paul McCartney fan so wanted to name his son after the musician. He quickly came to his senses, alas, meaning Wayne's household doesn't include a little lad named Macca Rooney.

WHEN DISCUSSING politics Willie Ferguson from Irvine admits he gets tongue tied. Though he knew exactly what he was saying when a colleague started pontificating on fisheries policy.

'You're talking a load of carp,' groaned Willie.

'I FELL in love with my girlfriend at second sight,' says Magnus Browne. 'The first time I met her I didn't know her father was a millionaire.'

A JOKE for those who like maths, booze or possibly both, from reader Charles Sullivan . . .

$f(x)=2x1$ walks into a bar.

The barman says:
  'Sorry, we don't cater for functions.'

A TALE of crackpot capitalism. Reader Paul Marshall said to the bloke serving at his local deli:
  'I'd like to buy a ham and cheese baguette with pickles.'
  'Sorry,' said the server, 'we only take cash or a card.'

'I GOT stung by nettles,' reveals reader Dan Ferguson. 'He charged me a hundred quid for a signed Bergerac DVD.'

A READER tells us of a speed-dating experience he had.

'Have you got any pets?' a young woman asked him.

'Yes,' he replied. 'A goldfish.'

'Any hobbies?' enquired the woman.

'Well,' said our reader, 'he does enjoy swimming . . .'

GRUMPY READER Martin Bonne says:

'Words can't express how much I hate Emoji Day.'

'I ASKED a German friend if he knew the square root of eighty-one,' says reader Scott Wace. Scott's German friend said . . .

'No.'

WHEN STILL Prime Minister, Boris Johnson intended to tackle the obesity crisis. Reader Frank Wilson believes the nation's obsession with pizza deliveries was to blame.

'The country's in the middle of a deep-pan demic,' he announced.

BOJO CONTINUED: The former PM decided to holiday in Scotland, where he wasn't massively popular.

'It's like Luke Skywalker packing his sun tan lotion and Speedos and heading to the Death Star for two weeks,' said reader Oliver Murray.

'MY ROOMMATE thinks our house is haunted,' says Graeme Harris. 'But I've lived here 400 years and never noticed a thing.'

SAINSBURY'S DECIDED to trial a virtual queue app which would enable shoppers to avoid hanging around outside the store. In a profound mood, reader Sonia Petersen says:

'Technology is just the knack of arranging the world so that you need not experience it.'

MUSING ABOUT the natural world, Coatbridge comedian Sam Tennent asks:

'Do you think whoever named the fly was gutted when he found out about birds?'

ONE OF our silliest contributors claimed to have been kidnapped by a group of mimes.

'They threatened to do unspeakable things to me,' he shuddered.

USEFUL CAREER advice from reader Hilary McGechie:

'If you're depressed about how little you've achieved up to now,' she says, 'remember that Bram Stoker didn't write Dracula until he was fifty. And Dracula didn't suck blood until he was dead.'

THE DIARY looks into the jaws of despair with the following traumatic tale. Reader Mary Hughes says:

'My extra sensitive toothpaste doesn't like it when I use other toothpastes.'

THERE ARE some great career paths to follow, explains reader Tom Staples, who tells us that his uncle works as a public relations manager for a company that makes bicycle wheels.

'He's the spokesman,' says Tom.

'THERE WAS once a Hollywood memorabilia auction which included some frantic bidding from Northern Ireland', reader Gordon McRae tells us. 'The lot in question was the sash Mia Farrow wore.'

BRACE YOURSELF, faithful reader. It's crackpot comment time. Reader Edward Travers tells us:

'The most gullible chemical element is easily lead.'

'AN INEBRIATED fellow is ambling home late one night,' reader Gordon Casely tells us. 'He halts when he spies a motorist leaning into the raised bonnet of his car to study the intricacies within.'

'What's up?' enquires the drunk.

'Piston broke,' answers the stranded driver.

'Same here,' admits the drunk.

BREAKING NEWS. Reader Dorothy Fowler informs us Donald Trump's library burned down. Both books were destroyed, and tragically, he hadn't finished colouring the second one.

CURIOUS ABOUT all things culinary, reader Paula Clark is eager to learn how to make ice-cream.

'I've decided to go to sundae school,' she says.

'WHAT PRIZE do you give someone who hasn't moved in a year?' asks Sue McGivern. 'A trophy.'

GLOBETROTTING GADABOUT Pete McNeill recalls a memorable visit to the UK capital.

'I shared a London taxi with a group of spotty youths,' he says. 'Must have been an acne carriage.'

'I'M INVITED to a hair-washing party,' says reader Sarah Winston. 'Now I can't think of a reason not to go.'

GOOD NEWS for reader Hugh Hamilton.

'My psychiatrist and I had a major breakthrough,' he beams. 'Now he can hear the voices, too.'

'IF A Tyrannosaurus Rex got a job manning a stall in the Barras,' muses reader Tim Croft, 'would that make it a small arms dealer?'

'WHICH TYPE of vegetable is only partially successful at being cool?' asks reader Wayne Richardson. 'The rad . . . ish, of course.'

3
CLIFF, ELVIS AND THE UPDATED NEWTONIAN LAWS OF PHYSICS

THE last section of this book dealt, in part, with monsters of one kind or another. We have to admit that the following chapter also has a few fearsome creatures . . . from the world of celebrity.

Of course, famous people don't gorge on blood like Dracula. They prefer to guzzle bottles of Dom Perignon. But don't underestimate the damage they can inflict upon the gentle and the innocent. Try and prevent a celeb swanking into the VIP

Lounge of a fashionable nightclub in Cannes and you will find yourself the recipient of a vengeful wrath that is both biblical and bitchy.

While perusing the following one-liners and gags you will witness Robbie Williams swaggering into view. Cliff Richard – the Grandpops of Pop – also makes an appearance. As does Elvis Presley, that dubious American rip-off version of Cliff.

We even have a joke about *Only Fools and Horses*, the greatest sitcom of all time (not to be named *Friends*, *The Office* or *Seinfeld*).

But it's not just the big shots you'll find in the following chapter. There are also quirky comments from – and about – the mere masses, i.e. the non-famous. Those shmucks who never win a Grammy, an Oscar, or even a Blue Peter badge.

Why are they included?

Because a great joke book should always be democratic in its daffiness and egalitarian when it comes to eejitry . . .

BREAKING NEWS. Reader Gordon Davies reveals that Robbie Williams has quit singing to become a geometry teacher.

'He's loving angles instead.'

'WHAT HAS ten teeth but two hundred legs?' asks reader Rab Briggs. 'The front row at a Cliff Richard concert.'

NEWS JUST in. Reader Jim Hamilton tells us:

'Because of covid, for the first time since 1945 the National Spelling Bee is cancil . . . cancul . . . cansel . . . it's called off.'

READER MAURICE Lochhead says the company he works for is better at making sun cream than its competitors.

'But I don't like to rub it in,' he adds.

SAFETY CONSCIOUS reader Simon Fowler uses a rubber Donald Trump facemask outdoors.

'It doesn't stop the transmission of respiratory droplets,' he concedes. 'On the other hand, people back off sharpish when they see me coming.'

A STORY of our times. After many years working on the waltzers and dodgems, reader Joe Knox was dismissed without notice.

'Should I now go to the tribunal claiming funfair dismissal?' he asks.

DIRE DAD anecdote.

'According to my wife I'm a rotten father for not treating my kids equally,' says reader Alex Brecker, who adds: 'I just don't understand it. I love Little Jimmy, Nicola and the ugly one all the same.'

A TEACHER asked her class why mobile phone masts could be bad for your health. After a lengthy pause, one pupil hesitantly answered:

'You might walk into it?'

A WARNING to all our readers from our traffic correspondent Bob Jamieson:

'A lorry carrying snooker equipment has crashed on the M74, spilling its load all over the carriageway.' Bob adds helpfully: 'There are cues in both directions.'

'APPARENTLY THERE'S a patron saint of security cameras,' reveals reader Anne Johnson. 'St Francis of a CCTV.'

'HOW DO you get a country girl's attention?' asks reader Adam Pottinger. 'Tractor.'

A DAFT funfair gag from Frank Owens from Baillieston about those curious folk who hang about tents.

'What's the best way to kill a circus?' he asks. 'Go for the juggler.'

A TRAGIC tale of marital disharmony. Reader Martin Grant's wife is throwing him out because of his *Only Fools and Horses* obsession.

'I'd better fetch the suitcase from the van,' he sighs.

'I BOOKED a limousine for £250 and found out that it doesn't come with a driver,' says reader Ken Miller. 'Can't believe I spent all that money with nothing to chauffeur it.'

FISHY PHILOSOPHISING from reader Adam Fern, who says:

'Give a man a fish and you will feed him for a day. But teach a man to fish and he will spend a fortune on gear he'll only use twice a year.'

KEEN HOBBYIST Tony Carr tells us:

'My obsession with coloured feathers is dyeing down.'

A SARTORIAL query from reader Derek Mitchell, who asks:

'Shouldn't tank tops offer more protection?'

THOUGHT FOR the day from reader Ronnie Gardener:

'"How old are you?" is literally the age-old question,' he points out.

MUSICAL THOUGHT for the day from reader Mark Pearce:

'If I sang a song about a sewing machine, would that make me a Singer songwriter?'

WE'RE NOT entirely sure we believe history buff Bill Henwick who tells us Elvis worked in the bomb disposal squad during his military service.

'It was because of his experience with suspicious mines,' adds our reader.

AS WIMBLEDON wends its way towards a conclusion, reader Gordon Wright tells us of two old gents watching the tennis on a pub TV.

Said one to the other:

'What's that bulge in the German player's pocket?'

'I think he's got a tennis ball there,' explained his friend.

'That can be sore,' noted the first chap. 'I had tennis elbow once.'

CONTEMPLATING PREJUDICES involved in the job market, Denis Bruce asks:

'Would a puppeteer ever pull strings to get a job?'

READER MATT Brown found himself struggling in his local library recently.

'I couldn't find a book on camouflage,' he sighs.

A FRUSTRATED Jim Hamilton gets in touch to demand that banks do a better job of keeping their ATMs replenished.

'I went to five in one day,' he grumps, 'and every one of them said insufficient funds.'

THE BATTLE of the sexes continues. Reader Jenny Coulter says:

'Women spend more time wondering what men are thinking than men spend actually thinking.'

SPOTTING A 'Fishing By Permit Only' sign, reader Alasdair MacKenzie was rather surprised.

'Here's me thinking I would need a rod,' he says.

A FEARFUL thought from reader Bob Murphy:

'"Do Not Touch!" must be the most terrifying thing to read in braille.'

SCIENTIFICALLY MINDED reader Matt Brown has updated a Newtonian law.

'For each action there is an equal and opposite reaction,' he says. 'Then a social media overreaction.'

A SILLY joke for chilly times.

'What do you call a snowman's temper tantrum?' asks reader Glenn Clarke. 'A meltdown.'

4
MIRTH (MINUS MYRTLE)

ERNEST HEMINGWAY was the sort of fellow who didn't believe in wasting a single word. His stories were as crisp and laconic as a message found inside a fortune cooky. He once managed to compose a six-word story, which he claimed was the best thing he ever wrote.

A great joke is very much like a Hemingway tale.

Taut.
To the point.
No excess flab or flannel.

For instance, that famous gag about the chicken who crosses the road. It doesn't supply any excess information, does it? What was the chicken's name, for instance? We never find out. (Though she was probably called Myrtle. Myrtle is a popular name in the chicken world.)

We also have scant information regarding the chicken's backstory. Did she have a happy childhood? What were her hopes and ambitions when she was a mere egg? Does she have a favourite member of the Beatles, or is she prog rockin' poultry?

None of these questions are answered by the joke. All we know for sure is that there is a chicken. And she's intent on crossing that road.

But what else do we really need to know? The beauty of a great gag lies in the editing process.

All excess info is chipped away. What remains is buffed and burnished until we are left with a hunk of pure humour.

That's exactly what you will find in the following tales, which are pithy to the point of perfection. So prepare yourself for Hemingwayesque yarns about dentistry, dog owners ... and an Alaskan eye doctor ...

EXASPERATED READER Pete McCourt has given up on keeping fit.

'The only way I'll get shredded at the gym is if my shoelace gets caught in the Stairmaster,' he sighs.

STAR WARS fan Malcolm Boyd was sad when David Prowse died, that towering chap who played lightsaber brandishing bad guy Darth Vader. Our reader says:

'I remember hearing that Darth Vader liked to spoil Luke Skywalker's Christmas fun by telling him that he had: "felt his presents."'

CYNICISM IS everywhere these days, though perhaps the most extreme case of this malady was witnessed by reader Helen Johnson.

'I once visited a planetarium,' she recalls, 'and somebody actually booed when they showed earth.'

AN UNLIKELY boast from reader Mal McCaffrey, who informs us that the inventor of the crossword puzzle lives near him.

'He's just three streets down and two across,' says Mal.

IT'S BEEN a rough financial year for reader Tom Stevens.

'I'm so poor my only funds are daylight savings from the summer,' he sighs.

WARNING. PROCEED with caution. The following tale involves a tragic event that may distress those who love cute animals, biscuits . . . or both.

Okay, still with us? Then reader Bob McGuinness has a story to tell.

'I bought a pack of those animal shaped biscuits,' says Bob, who adds glumly: 'but I had to take them back. The seal was broken.'

IT'S LUCKY that Fife comedian Richard Pulsford is a talented stand-up, because his attempts to change career have sadly come to naught.

'I've received a rejection letter from NASA,' says Richard. 'Strangely, it says there's no space on their training programme.'

'AN OLD friend of mine turned out to be a backstabber,' says reader Pete Harris. 'Or as he calls it, an acupuncturist.'

IN A cruel mood, reader Eric Hill says he has changed his name on Facebook to 'No one'. He adds:

'Now when I see idiotic posts I can click "like" and it will say, "No one likes this".'

A NASTY joke about a mime from reader Hugh Peebles.

'How do you shoot a mime?' he asks. 'With a silencer.'

'I JUST watched a film about a man with a broken leg,' says reader Tom Willetts. 'Great cast.'

SOPHISTICATED READER Tom Platt wants to buy old copies of *Classical Music Magazine*.

'I'm looking for Bach issues,' he explains.

DAFT ADVICE of the day from reader Dave Nicholls, who says:

'If a lamppost disappears on your street you can always pin a "missing" message on a cat.'

'IT'S TIME to update the vernacular,' argues reader Tim James. 'From now on I'm calling TV dinners satellite dishes.'

WHILE ON a stroll reader Michael Lynch claims to have come across a young lady running a battery kiosk in the local park.

'She sells C cells by the seesaw,' says Michael.

'WHAT DO you call a native Alaskan eye doctor?' asks reader Paul Miller. 'An optical Aleutian.'

DISMISSIVE READER Ian Stuart says winning the Dentist of the Year award is no big deal, explaining:

'All you get is a little plaque.'

'I PHONED the Impatience Sufferers Hotline the other day,' says reader Pete Thompson. 'They put me in the back of the queue.'

AN UNLIKELY story from reader Gwen Stewart, who says:

'I didn't believe this bloke I met who told me that he was a pop star from the 1980s. But he was adamant.'

CRAFTY CANINE owner Scott Merton says:

'I named my dog "Five Miles". Now I tell people I walk Five Miles twice a day.'

THOUGHTFUL READER Iain Lucas says:

'Why do we use the phrase emotional baggage? It should be griefcase.'

RYANAIR BOSS Michael O'Leary strolls into a pub after a hard day at his UK office and asks for a pint of Guinness. As the barman is pouring he says:

'That'll be fifty pence, please.'

An impressed O'Leary replies:

'That's very cheap. Great!'

'Ah,' says the barman: 'But you'll be wanting a glass.'

'MY WIFE asked me to stop singing Wonderwall,' says reader Doug McAdams. 'I said maybe . . .'

TECHNOLOGICALLY SAVVY reader Keith Duncan says:

'Apparently you can't use "beef stew" as a password. It's not stroganoff.'

COCKAMAMIE COMMENT time.

'What's the leading cause of dry skin?' asks Rob Castle. 'Towels.'

THINKING OF the feathered creatures of the sky reminds Russell Smith from Largs of the tale of the homing pigeon that was late back.

'It was such a nice day he decided to walk,' says Russell.

'I WISH Medusa would stop objectifying people,' says reader Neil Black.

'I WENT to a pub called The Light Brigade,' says reader Callum Shaw. 'They certainly know how to charge.'

DAFT JOKE time. 'Where does a dog go when his tail falls off?' asks reader Charles Roberts. 'A retailers, of course.'

A CURIOUS query from reader Don Preston, who says:

'If a human cannonball loses his job, does that mean he isn't fired?'

AN UNLIKELY story from reader Walter Perry, who says:

'I bought a new plane the other day. Disappointed they didn't let me keep the hanger.'

'WAS THERE ever a more ground-breaking invention than the shovel?' enquires reader Bob McPake.

'I USED to love eating chips,' says reader Dan Kent. 'But then they threw me out of the casino.'

A TRICKY question from a reader, who asks:

'What word becomes shorter when you add two letters to it?' The answer, of course, is: 'Short.'

JADED READER Danielle Norris says:

'If you've seen one shopping centre, you've seen a mall.'

A STORY about a relationship gone awry. Reader John Bryson tells us his girlfriend wanted to split up because he was always acting like a detective. To which John responded:

'Good idea. We can cover more ground that way.'

'WHAT DO you get if you divide the circumference of an apple by its diameter?' asks Marc Portis. 'Apple pi.'

'IF YOU'RE not supposed to eat at night,' says a reader, 'why is there a light bulb in the refrigerator?'

'I DELETED all the German names from my pre-owned mobile phone,' says reader Garry Roberts. 'It's now Hans free.'

'I LIKE the word "tinnitus",' says reader Ralph Jamieson. 'It has a nice ring to it.'

IN AN inspirational mood, reader Jim Hamilton says:

'Whatever you do, always give 100% ... unless you're donating blood.'

'I LOVE playing chess with people I meet in the park,' says reader David Marshall. 'Though sometimes it's not easy finding thirty-two of them willing to take part.'

5
THE CASUAL CRUELTY OF TOP TENNIS PROFESSIONALS

MAKING a blockbuster movie is a simple thing to do. All you need is a good story to tell. A clapperboard.

And a few million quid in the bank.

That's what legendary film director Francis Ford Coppola discovered this year when he decided to work on a longstanding dream project of his called *Megalopolis*.

The man behind *The Godfather* and *Apocalypse Now* was forced to concede that he would have to use one hundred million bucks of his own money to get the film into production. Of course, he could have made the film for slightly less dosh if he had changed its name from *Megalopolis* to *Teenytinyopolis*.

But Coppola would never make such a concession. He's a chap who needs to celebrate his grand, sweeping vision of the world.

This joke book also has a grand, sweeping vision of the world. In the following chapter we bound effortlessly from a brutal martial arts scene to the romance of Balmoral. Andy Murray even makes a guest appearance, and we didn't have to pay him for his services.

That's the great thing about a joke book. It's cheaper to produce than a Francis Ford Coppola epic. Yet you still end up with the same amount of thrills, chills and spills.

(Note to readers: While it's true that the creators of this joke book are in no desperate need of extra cash, if you *do* happen to find one hundred million quid down the back of your sofa, we will be delighted to invest it wisely, with the help of our favourite turf accountant.)

'I TRIED chatting with my wife while she applied a mud mask,' says reader David Weaver 'you should have seen the filthy look she gave me.'

SPORT-LOVING READER Gordon Wright tells us the following tale:

'Two cats are looking in a sport shop window. One says to the other:

"My brother's in that racket."'

GETTING OLD: the facts. Reader Alfred Green says:

'I'm at that age when I can only enjoy Alphabetti Spaghetti with my reading glasses on.'

LACKING ENERGY, reader William Hough quit working as a personal trainer.

'I handed in my too weak notice,' he says.

'MY SECRET is that I'm addicted to seaweed,' says reader Eleanor Briggs. 'I need kelp.'

A READER once told us this tale of tragedy in the 1960s:

'Why didn't the lifeguard save the hippy? He was too far out, man.'

YET AGAIN we dare to tackle the most contentious questions of our era, with Eric Arbuckle from Largs demanding to know,

'If one enjoys a jam sandwich whilst wearing a sleeveless jacket, would this be a gilet piece?'

USEFUL ADVICE from reader Lynn Thomas, who says:

'Never ask an English teacher who has just been released from jail to marry you. They will always explain that you can't end a sentence with a proposition.'

STUDYING HIS family history, reader Tom Evans made a startling discovery.

'I come from a long line of conga dancers,' he reveals.

NATURAL HISTORY correspondent David Shaw gets in touch to tell us that the swordfish has no natural predators.

'Except for the penfish,' he adds, most authoritatively.

READER GEORGE Campbell supplies us with the following bit of daftness . . .

It seems there was a poor wee mutt who lost his tail in an accident.

'Did it spoil his carriage?' a concerned friend enquired of the owner.

'Don't know about his carriage,' came the reply. 'But it sure wrecked his wagon.'

GENEROUS FATHER Walter Hodgkinson gave his son a flat piece of cardboard for his birthday.

'Well, he did say he wanted an ex box,' explains Walter.

DUBIOUS CONTACT Bob Fowler says:

'I'm selling a broken pub quiz machine online. No questions asked.'

FORGING A career in fungus identification is rather dull, claims reader Russell Boyd:

'Every day, it's just say mould, say mould.'

EMPOWERING THOUGHT for the day from reader Carl Farmer:

'You'll never be as lazy as the bloke who named the fireplace.'

QUESTION: WHAT do you call it when a foolish fellow decides to place a bet on the highly unlikely event of Croatia beating Scotland in a footy match?

ANSWER: 'Quid pro Cro'.

'SOME PEOPLE don't like ring-shaped islands,' notes reader Stan Phillips. 'But I think they're not bad atoll.'

FILM FAN Norman Powell tells us that movie icon and martial artist Bruce Lee had a brother who was even faster with his fists. His name? Sudden Lee, of course.

EVER WONDERED why some brides weep at their own wedding? Reader Lucy Webb has a theory.

'It's because they never get to marry the best man,' she explains.

'IF YOU can't hear a pin drop,' says reader Scott Wright, 'something is clearly wrong with your bowling.'

'WHAT DO you give the woman or man who has everything?' asks reader Liz Dale. 'Antibiotics.'

WE SALUTE Andy Murray, a chap who has always performed minor miracles on the lawns of Wimbledon. Though reader Frank Galbraith isn't impressed by tennis players as a group.

'The divorce rate is very high amongst their ilk,' he points out . . . 'To them, love means nothing.'

A GRAMMATICAL point, made with some gravitas, by reader Maurice Bonner, who says:

'In the old days, excessive use of commas was considered to be a serious crime. It usually resulted in a long sentence.'

'IT TAKES about five years for a walnut tree to produce nuts,' says Sid Leslie from Kirkintilloch, who adds: 'In my experience, a family tree is much more efficient in this area.'

A MEDICAL malady. Reader Pete Watson says:

'I'm taking steps to deal with my escalator phobia.'

'IF YOU drive an electric car you'll need a current licence,' points out reader Douglas Roy.

THOUGHT FOR the day from reader Tam Miller:

'Refusing to accept Darwin's Theory of Evolution is proof that the theory is correct and you are trapped at Stage 1.'

A TOP tip from reader Bill Cassidy:

'Always keep an empty milk carton in the fridge, just in case someone pops in and asks for a black coffee.'

'BALMORAL HAVE launched two new varieties of gin,' notes Norman McAllister from Hamilton. 'At £30 and £60 a bottle, I expect they'll get off to a sloe start.'

'I'M THINKING about installing a *Lord of the Rings* themed kitchen,' says reader Theresa Scott. 'Apparently it has a great hob bit.'

READER ROBIN Gilmour informs us that his wife is threatening to leave him because of his obsession with football.

'I'm gutted,' sighs Robin. 'After all, we've been together seven seasons.'

THE DEMANDS of the carnivorous diet. Reader Henry Murray points out:

'When you choke on a piece of meat, it's that animal's last chance at revenge.'

SOME IMPORTANT marital advice from reader Willie Campbell, who says:

'The first rule of monogamy is do no harem.'

'LIGHT TRAVELS faster than sound,' points out reader Roberta Ward. 'That's why some people appear bright before you hear them speak.'

SOME PEOPLE are glass half-full types. Some are glass half-empty. Reader Richard Moore says:

'I exclusively use plastic Tupperware receptacles, so I'm not sure where that leaves me.'

6
ENTER KERMIT

THE Muppets were the breakout megastars of the 1970s (if you don't include Jack Nicholson, Led Zeppelin and the Blue Peter double-act of Shep and his loyal chum, John Noakes). From 1974 until '75, Kermit, Miss Piggy and the rest of the gang starred in their own popular television programme... *The Muppet Show*.

Even though they were huge stars, the Muppets could never quite evade the acrid whiff of scandal that followed in their wake. The whispers were insistent and insidious. Were the posse of primetime entertainers really 'Muppets' as they so confidently claimed? Or perhaps – as was oft muttered in secretive Hollywood circles – were they actually, y'know, just puppets, like Basil Brush, Sooty or some old sock with googly eyes attached?

For many years, investigative reporters tried to discover the truth of this shocking allegation. But Kermit – that sly old ribbiter – continued to keep schtum. Even when confronted by the threat of a fashionable Parisian chef wielding a pair of scissors in one hand, and a recipe for Cuisses de Grenouille in the other.

As you probably have realised by now, at least one of the Muppets will make a guest appearance in the following chapter. Though we can't promise to solve any mysteries regarding the DNA of these curious celebrity creatures.

This is a joke book, after all. If you want the empirical sifting of scientific data, you're probably best reading one of those weighty tomes written by A. Einstein or S. Hawking.

Though be warned. Those books have hardly any jokes. And the Muppets never appear.

Not even once.

THOUGHT FOR the day from reader Raymond Harris, who says:

'Being ambivalent has its pros and cons.'

'HOW DO you cut the ocean in half?' asks reader Bob Rushton. 'With a sea-saw, of course.'

IN THE hushed tones of David Attenborough creeping through the African veldt, reader Ted Fisher gets in touch to educate us in the ways of the wild.

'If pelicans weren't optimistic,' he points out, 'they'd be called pelicants.'

WHEN READER Darren Anderson received an email explaining how to read maps backwards, he was intrigued.

'Turns out it was just spam,' he sighs.

'I HEARD a rumour Greggs were starting home deliveries using drones,' says reader Malcolm Boyd. 'Sounds a bit pie in the sky to me.'

SUGGESTION OF the day from reader Paul Simpson:

'A good sign for a strip club during the daytime would be: "Sorry, we're clothed."'

'BECOMING A vegetarian is one big missed steak,' points out carnivorous reader Scott Jones.

AN INTRIGUING thought from reader Ben Travers, who says:

'I wonder if people in lightbulb factories feel any pressure to come up with new ideas.'

'I SWAPPED my Xbox for a quarter pound of venison,' reveals Stevie Campbell from Hamilton: 'My wife's not too pleased, but I told her it's a definite game changer.'

COMMERCIALLY MINDED reader Colin Harris says:

'I've just sold my homing pigeon on eBay. For the twenty-second time.'

'I'VE AN electrician friend who used to be a police detective,' says reader Maurice Owen. 'We call him Sherlock Ohms.'

BOASTFUL READER John Moore tells us:
  'I was recently voted time traveller of the year 2172.'

ANIMAL LOVING Arthur Bowden fancies a job looking after Australian marsupials at Edinburgh Zoo.
  'Unfortunately,' he sighs, 'I don't possess the necessary koalafications.'

'DID MY first nude painting this morning,' boasts reader Tom Atherton. 'The neighbours weren't delighted but the front door looks terrific.'

MULLING OVER the future, reader Sue Holloway predicts there will be a baby boom a few months from now:

'So in the year 2034 we'll have to deal with the "quaranteens."'

DAFT GAG time. Reader Hugh Peebles wonders if we know what you call a Scotsman with one foot inside his house and one foot outside.

'Hame-ish, of course.'

THOUGHT FOR the day from reader Daniel Fletcher, who says:

'The heart is such a strong muscle because it's constantly pumping iron.'

'I GOT fed up working at a sausage factory,' says reader Alex Martin. 'I just sat there staring at the Wall's.'

GHOULISH GAG time.

'I enjoyed an evening out at an Autopsy Club,' says Kevin Arnold. 'It was Open Mike night.'

AN EXCEEDINGLY silly joke a reader once told us:

'What's orange and sounds like a parrot? A carrot, of course.'

USEFUL ADVICE about extending your lifespan from reader Arnold Garner:

'If the Grim Reaper knocks on your front door, fend him off with a vacuum cleaner. Dyson with death may be your only chance . . .'

CURIOUS STEVIE Campbell from Hamilton wonders if it's true that when students at Glasgow School of Art approached the board asking for information about the future of the fire damaged building they were told to:

'Draw their own conclusions.'

A QUALITY quirky question from reader Paul Murphy:

'If I yelled into a colander would that strain my voice?'

KEEN WILDLIFE observer Ken Mitchell says:

'Elephants use their trunks to breathe while in water, so technically, they're swimming trunks.'

FEELING HIS age, reader Alex Hargrave says:

'I'm old enough to remember when emojis were called hieroglyphics.'

ENTREPRENEURIAL CORRESPONDENT Paul H Costello is thinking about starting his own tree felling business.

'There'll be branches everywhere,' he boasts.

AN INSPIRATIONAL tale of overcoming adversity with pluck and determination from reader David Lawrence.

'I couldn't figure out seatbelts for a long time,' he explains. 'Then it just clicked.'

'I HANDED my dad his fiftieth birthday card,' says reader Scott Cronin, who adds: 'Dad said one card would have been enough.'

A JOKE that has a punchline and a (possible) puppet. What more could you possibly want? Roderick Archibald Young asks:

'What did Kermit the frog say when he got to the top of the hill?' The answer is: 'A Muppet.'

THINKING ABOUT Dominic Cummings, Boris Johnson's former controversial advisor, reader Jim Morrison says:

'It wasn't the Cummings that got him in trouble. It was the goings.'

HAVING A go at humbleness, reader Gavin White says:

'Someone a lot smarter than me once said feigned humility is endearing.'

PSYCHOLOGICAL SILLINESS from reader Martin Franzen.

'Why was Ivan Pavlov's hair so soft?' he asks. 'Because he conditioned it.'

AN ACUTE culinary comment from reader Maria Roberts:

'If you eat an entire cake without cutting it you technically only had one piece.'

A SLIVER of silliness from Martin Pierce, who says:

'My pal David had his ID stolen. Now he's just Dav.'

STATISTICAL ANALYSIS from reader Ed Barker, who tells us:

'There are two types of people in this world.

1) Those who can extrapolate from incomplete data.'

GOOFY GAG time.

'What do you call a fish with no eyes?' asks Pete Evans. 'Fsh.'

7
MARITAL STRIFE, DEADLY PIANOS AND OTHER CHARMING TALES

IN many ways humour is like a jar of gherkins. And not just any jar of gherkins. A jar of gherkins where the lid has been unscrewed, a grubby hand has rummaged around in the pickle brine, and one or two gherkins have been well-and-truly nibbled. That sort of jar of gherkins has an exceedingly brief shelf life. It's liable to turn 'Yeuch!' at any moment.

Humour also has a brief shelf life. What seems hilarious one day is excruciatingly unfunny the next. Take Charlie Chaplin, for instance. In the early years of the last century he was the king of comedy; an artist of amiable anarchy.

Watch a Chaplin flick today, however, and what do you get? A moustache. A bowler hat. And not one giggle in sight.

You may wonder how we managed to keep the gags in this book so fresh, so frisky, so fun. Well, for a start we dipped the book in an exceedingly large jar of pickle brine, then made sure not to unscrew the lid until publication was imminent.

Even more important, we made sure each joke has a topical sting . . . of sorts. For instance, in the following chapter we have a gag about boomerangs, which are very contemporary. After all, nothing is as technologically advanced as a slightly bent stick of wood.

We also have a rib-tickler about exorcism, a vogue subject if ever there was one ... if you happen to be a priest living in Medieval Europe.

Okay, perhaps the following jokes aren't exactly tip-top topical. But they will still give you a laugh-and-a-half (and sometimes even a laugh-and-three-quarters. That's the kind of value we supply).

And best of all?

We promise no moustaches or bowler hats. (They'd just get soggy in the pickle brine.)

A SPORTING admission from reader Nigel Morton:

'If there's one thing that makes me throw up, it's a dartboard on the ceiling.'

A GRAMMATICAL thought from reader Ted Hardman:

'Good punctuation is a sentence that's well written and bad punctuation is a sentence that's, well, written.'

'WHAT DO you call a boomerang that doesn't return?' asks Kevin Barker. 'A stick.'

'I GOT a loan to pay for an exorcism,' explains Martin Lee. 'If I don't pay it back I'll be repossessed.'

A TALE of marital strife.

'My wife accused me of being immature,' reveals reader Rob McCoy, who adds: 'I fired back that she was insensitive for climbing into my treehouse without using the secret password.'

A THEATRICAL lesson from reader Stephen Thompson.

'Why do we tell actors to break a leg?' he asks. 'Because every play has a cast.'

A DAFFY doggy story.

'What do you call a man with small feet and no dog?' enquires Gordon Wright. 'Wee Shoey Dugless.'

THE WIFE of reader Rob Linford claims he's greedy. To prove her wrong he's taking her out for tea and biscuits.

'It's bound to be a special day,' says Rob. 'She's never given blood before.'

BREAKING NEWS. Reader Tim Curran informs us that scientists have announced they have invented a car fuelled by parsley.

'They're now working on a train that runs on thyme,' he adds.

'A FRIEND passed his degree in sound engineering,' says reader Chris Austin. 'He got a 1-2-1-2.'

'THE BEST time to add insult to injury is when you're signing somebody's cast,' points out reader Vic Crawford.

A TALE of health care and hostelries. Christopher Ide from East Renfrewshire tells us of a registered medical practitioner who strolls into a bar and asks for a daiquiri cocktail. The barman mixes the ingredients and sprinkles grated hickory into the drink. Handing it over, he says:

'Here's your hickory daiquiri, doc.'

'**I THREW** a surprise house-warming party for my Inuit chum,' says reader Colin Young. 'Now he's homeless.'

WE NOW present an epic narrative crackling with dramatic energy.

'I asked an electrician to sort out a problem in my house,' says reader Gareth Murray. 'He refused.'

'**IF YOU** got a job running Old Macdonald's farm, would that make you the CIEIO?' wonders reader Dan Burton.

'**I USED** to sit next to a boy who spent all day counting,' says reader Barry Clarke. 'I wonder what he's up to now?'

A SAD note. The uncle of reader Peter Duffy was crushed by a piano.

'His funeral was very low key,' sobs Peter.

'I HAD to give up my business plan to make worksurfaces for shops,' sighs reader Mike Rhoden. 'It was proving to be counterproductive.'

AMBITIONS CAN be crushing when they don't come to fruition, as reader Mike Priestley knows.

'I harboured an unrealistic dream of becoming a mathematician,' he reveals. 'Guess that was just pi in the sky.'

AMBITIOUS READER Mark Wilson says:

'I've set myself a five-year plan to be more spontaneous.'

DAFFY DETECTIVE joke from reader Ken Campbell, who asks:

'What is Sherlock Holmes' favourite type of rock?' The answer, is of course . . . 'It's sedimentary, my dear Watson.'

A CULINARY query from reader Ed Bilton, who wants to know why the American term for chips is 'French fries'.

'It's obvious that they're not cooked in France,' says Ed. 'They're cooked in grease.'

THOUGHT FOR the day from reader David Donaldson, who asks:

'Do the inhabitants of Woking show a particularly high level of political consciousness?'

WHEN IT comes to tall tales, this joke book doesn't footer about. So without further ado, we present Stevie Campbell from Hamilton, who explains:

'I once tried to pay my chiropodist with a fake £20 note. Unfortunately she spotted this immediately and told me it was counterfeet. I fainted at this point and ended up comatoes.'

'I REALLY wanted to vent my spleen,' admits *River City* actor Sanjeev Kohli. 'In the end I got a fan fitted to my liver.'

INSTEAD OF a swear jar, reader Tim Blunden has a negativity jar.

'When I have a pessimistic thought I put a pound in it,' he says. 'It's half empty.'

A PHILOSOPHICAL thought from reader Julie Baldwin:

'If Pinocchio was real, a corrupt joiner would have stolen him by now to use as an infinite source of free wood.'

WHEN READER Geoff Gordon slips his mortal coil, he wants to be buried with his record collection.

'It'll be my vinyl resting place,' he says.

'THEY SAY the camera adds ten pounds,' notes reader Albert Fowler, 'so I've started taking photos of my wallet.'

'I NEED to visit the garden centre so I can grow my own herbs,' admits reader Pete Miller. 'I've been living on borrowed thyme.'

A QUIRKY query from reader Gwen Thomas, who asks:

'Is a baby porcupine the pre-quill to an adult porcupine?'

MUSIC-LOVING DENIS Bruce from Bishopbriggs wonders:

'Could a singer who is confused about their identity have an alto ego?'

ADDING FURTHER complications to the above debate, a reader demands to know:

'Does an ordained minister have an altar ego?'

MORE OF the same. A reader contributes to the above mystery by asking:

'Does a quadruped have a halter ego?'

AN UNLIKELY tale from reader Sandy Stewart, who claims to have taken the shell off his racing snail to make him go faster.

'If anything, it made him more sluggish,' says a despondent Sandy.

'THE ONLY difference between clutching a ball in your hands and doing a handstand is you're just holding a bigger ball ... called Earth,' notes reader Ted Ivory.

8
A TORTOISE, A HARE
AND SIR ELTON JOHN

MANY books throughout history have fired the flames of controversy. James Joyce's *Ulysses* was banned in numerous countries because of its super-saucy content (and we don't mean that each book came with a free sachet of ketchup).

For much the same reason *Lady Chatterley's Lover* by D.H. Lawrence had large numbers of readers swooning all the way to the smelling salts, suffering from a most disagreeable case of the vapours.

Even in our modern era books have continued to be labelled scandalous. Literary works such as *A Clockwork Orange* and *The Wasp Factory* both caused distress because of their visceral, violent content.

Brace yourself, gentle reader. For the volume which you currently hold in your hands is also highly controversial. For it is a gag book. Yet it doesn't include any knock-knock jokes (put the book down now if you must. Race for those smelling salts).

We did consider including a few knock-knocks. After all, they have a certain amount of dramatic tension, especially at the commencement of each story. You know how it goes:

'Good gracious! Is that somebody knocking? At *my* door? Whoever can it be?!'

But in other respects, knock-knock jokes are a tad outdated. After all, who chooses to bruise their knuckles thumping on a wooden door when, in all likelihood, there is a serviceable doorbell merely inches away?

So, knock-knock . . . no thank you.

But don't feel too bereft. For we do have Elton John in this chapter. And he's more entertaining than any wooden entranceway you care to mention.

Plus, the tortoise and the hare are just about to come lolloping into view. Though our analysis of their individual natures may not be what you're expecting . . .

ROCK ICONS don't like to be kept waiting. So let's bring Sir Elton on immediately, courtesy of a comment from reader Rab Fulton, who says:

'I used to wonder if Elton John liked lettuce. Then I realised he was a rocket man.'

PHILOSOPHICAL READER Joanna Brett says:

'The moral of the Tortoise and the Hare is not "slow and steady wins the race". It's "big-eared carrot addict shouldn't blow his lead by showing off".'

INTRIGUING READER Graeme Jones says:

'There's only one thing worse than leaving someone in suspense . . .'

THOUGHTFUL READER Will Brenner says:

'It's very easy to turn a regular sofa into a sofa bed. All you have to do is forget your wife's birthday.'

BROWSING IN a charity shop, reader Gordon Murray spotted an ancient book titled: *A Guide to Surgical Procedures.* Our reader adds:

'Perhaps not surprisingly the appendix was missing.'

AMATEUR METEOROLOGIST Deborah Steele wonders:

'If the temperature is zero outside today, and it's twice as cold tomorrow, how cold will it be?'

'**I ORDERED** a book online called *How to Scam People*,' says reader Oliver Jones, who adds: 'That was four months ago. It still hasn't arrived.'

THE DIARY presents a dramatic vignette involving cosmetic dentistry and a Central European nation, courtesy of reader Maurice Doyle...

Maurice said to his dentist:
  'I want my teeth whiter.'

The dentist said:
  'Have you tried polish?'

Maurice said:
  'Chcieć moich zębów biały.'

His dentist ignored him.

'I TRAINED my dog to fetch beer,' says reader Grant Watson. 'It may not sound that impressive, but he gets them from the neighbour's fridge.'

PHILOSOPHICAL THOUGHT from reader David Garner:

'Why do people pay to go up tall buildings then put money in binoculars to look at things on the ground?'

ON HIS first visit back to the gym, Sandy Tuckerman hoped to shift some flab. Though he was put off somewhat by the nincompoop on the exercise bike next to his, who had placed a bottle of water in the Pringles holder.

SOME THOUGHTFUL advice from reader Ted Edwyn, who says:

'If you see someone wearing camouflage, make sure to walk right into them, so they know it's working.'

AN UNLIKELY tale from reader Ted Marshall:

'I met my wife on the net. We were both bad trapeze artists.'

EXHAUSTED READER Ian Watson nodded off while eating a plate of rice.

'I was asleep as soon as my head hit the pilau,' he says.

DEPRESSED READER Stan Cooper cheered himself up by comfort eating.

'Now my breath smells of fabric conditioner,' he sighs.

KEEN TO educate herself, reader Christine Cochrane took a course in the visual arts.

'But I didn't complete my homework,' she sighs. 'So I had to drop out of collage.'

ESSENTIAL FARMYARD information from reader Ralph Duffy:

'Why do cows have hooves instead of feet?' asks Ralph. 'Because they lactose.'

BOARDGAME AFICIONADO Roger McEvoy claims there will never be an edible version of Scrabble.

'If there is,' he adds, 'I'll eat my words.'

A SAD yet happy story from reader Ed Houston, who tells us:

'I was delighted when someone stole my flashlight.'

CURIOUS READER Neil Byrne asks:

'Before Jeff Bezos goes to bed does he put his pajamazon?'

'MY TEENAGE son treats me like I'm a god,' says reader Roberta Richardson. 'He acts like I don't exist until he wants something.'

CURIOUS READER Pete Setterfield says:

'Do you think the word "subtle" has a "b" because someone snuck it in there in an understated fashion?'

INSPIRATIONAL READER Chis Hill boasts:

'I've decided to follow my dreams. I'll be spending more time in bed.'

BAR-ROOM BADINAGE from reader Tom Randall.

'Three conspiracy theorists walk into a pub,' says Tom. 'Don't tell me it was a coincidence.'

CONFUSED READER Claire Bisset admits:

'When it comes to messing up simple sayings, I've been there, done that, got the tea bag.'

'I MET a microbiologist recently,' says reader Harry Amery. 'He was much bigger than I expected.'

'I EXPLAINED to my suitcase that we aren't going on holiday this year,' says reader Ted Jeffrey. 'Now I'm dealing with emotional baggage.'

'MY WIFE wondered if our kids were spoiled,' says reader Colin Murphy. 'I told her most kids smell that way.'

AS A youngster, reader Ramsey Travers dreamed of being a snooker player.

'Unfortunately, I never got my big break,' he sighs.

QUICK-WITTED READER Harry Amery asks:
  'If you chat up a sprinter, does that mean you're trying to pull a fast one?'

AN ECONOMIC query from reader Bill Ferguson:
  'If a Domino's Pizza restaurant goes bust, do the other restaurants in the chain then go bust, one after the other?'

FRUSTRATED READER George Grant tells us:
  'I tried to find a pun about carpentry. But nothing wood work.'

A PROFOUND thought from reader Robin Gilmour, who tells us:
  'Bread is like the sun. It rises in the yeast and sets in the waist.'

AMBITIOUS BOB Wallace wanted to start a colorectal consultancy:

'Then I realised I'd have to start at the bottom and work my way up.'

9
THE WORST GAG EVER (PLUS SOME SWINGIN' COOL CATS)

THE problem with jokes is that they always have to compete with the real world. And sometimes the real world is funnier than anything you could possibly make up.

Take this year's Met Gala in New York, for instance. A sparkling affair that was described as the fashion event of the season. In other words, it was a bunch of well-connected folk plus celebs wearing ultra-expensive hats, shoes, frocks and trousers.

And just to make things a tad confusing, the hats were often worn as shoes, while the frocks and trousers dripped from the wrists like bangles.

But that's high fashion, da'ling. And if you dare to chuckle at the eccentric antics on display, it merely means you're a member of the hoi polloi from Planet Hicksville, with no understanding of the world of hotshot and hipster (you knuckle-dragging oik, you).

At this year's shimmering shindig some people even arrived wearing costumes that prominently displayed labels attacking the mega rich. Inevitably it was the mega rich who wore these lavish creations.

Nobody else could afford them.

See what we mean? The Met Gala is reality (or some people's reality). Yet it's also a joke. And a delicious one, at that. So how is it possible to top the high society hilarity of the majestically mockable Met?

In the following chapter we certainly give it a try. And, hey, Bing Crosby, Frank Sinatra and Tony Bennett are just about to arrive on the scene.

Now what could be swisher or sweller than those fine fellers?

FIENDISHLY CUNNING reader Bert Forbes has devised the perfect way to get ahead in life:

'I learn from the mistakes of people who have taken my advice.'

GREEN-FINGERED READER Dennis Simpson intends to visit his local garden centre, as he needs a gizmo to do some snippety-snipping in the area surrounding his lawn.

'I want the most modern implement there is,' he says. 'It has to be cutting hedge technology.'

MEDICAL EXPERT Anne Lennon gets in touch to explain that a doctor who specialises in Adam's apples is a 'guyneckologist'.

WE ARE always sad when one of our correspondents is laid low by illness. John Mulholland recently noticed that whenever he hears songs by the likes of Bing Crosby, Frank Sinatra and Tony Bennett he gets a headache and a pain in the ears.

'I reckon I've got crooner virus,' he sighs.

A LANARKSHIRE reader transfixed by political turmoil in Holyrood recalls a comment made by an after-dinner speaker:

'All politicians are like bananas,' he said. 'They go in green, turn yellow and are bent.'

READER PAUL Fowler asks:

'Does anyone really care if scientists find a cure for apathy?'

CURIOUS READER Ian Grimmer asks:

'When the person who was designing the drawing board got it wrong, what did they go back to?'

ANOTHER DOGGY tale. Former Labour MP Jim McGovern tells us of a chap who arranges to meet his friend in the pub at 2pm, though the friend doesn't arrive until three.

'Sorry I'm late,' he says. 'Just playing a couple of hands of poker with my dog.'

'Wow!' says the first bloke. 'Your dog plays poker? He must be smart.'

'Not really,' says the friend. 'Every time he gets a good hand he wags his tail.'

OUR GENEROUS readers are always enthusiastic when it comes to backing good causes. For instance, Martin Ross from Neilston tells us:

'Next week I'll be attending an animal rights barbeque . . . yum!'

DAFT QUESTION of the day from reader Roger Conner:

'What do you call a beat-up Batman? Bruised Wayne, of course.'

SILLY JOKE time.

'What names did the drummer give his twin daughters?' asks reader Shirley Munro. 'Anna 1. Anna 2.'

BIRDWATCHER JOHN Wright points out that you very rarely see owls getting amorous in the rain.

'It's too wet to woo,' he says.

DAFT QUESTION of the day from reader Ken Summers, who asks which colour can open your vehicle. The answer is, of course, 'Khaki'.

'I TRIED to shave with a Bic,' explains reader Mike Brunton. 'Bad mistake. Got ink all over my chin.'

'I WANTED to send Bugs Bunny a letter,' says reader Bill Glover, 'but the only way he communicates is through a WhatsApp Doc.'

QUESTION OF the day from reader Pete Miller, who says:

'If an apple a day keeps the doctor away, why don't Daleks hide in orchards?'

'SOMEONE HAS been dumping soil in my garden,' says reader Ralph Pearson. 'The plot thickens . . .'

ESSENTIAL DIETARY advice from reader Gordon Casely, who says:

'By replacing your morning coffee with green tea, you can lose up to 87 per cent of what little joy you still have left in your life.'

THE WORD 'yuck' is used as an expression of profound disgust, though in America it also means to laugh heartily at something. Reader Hugh Peebles manages to combine the two by informing us of the humorously horrid conclusion he arrived at after suffering from an upset stomach.

'Diarrhoea is hereditary,' he sighs. 'It runs in the jeans.'

FINANCIALLY MINDED reader Gary Milton asks:

'Pickpocketing. Is it the earliest type of crowdfunding?'

FRUSTRATED READER Pat Hogan got stuck in a traffic jam the other day. He says:

'I was there for so long that even the satnav said 'Are we there yet?''

DAVID RUSSELL from Penicuik proudly presents the following as the worst gag ever (he heard it from a chap feeding the animals at Glasgow Zoo years ago, so we'll blame him instead of David).

'Why do polar bears prefer Glasgow Zoo to Edinburgh Zoo? Because it's a Calderpark.'

ON A similar topic, reader John Cochrane says:

'If a gnu was introduced to a Scottish zoo would it be named Hawkeye (the gnu)?'

EDINBURGH COMEDIAN Martin Bearne is feeling disappointed with himself.

'I can't believe I didn't figure out I was colour blind,' he says. 'I never should have ignored all those blue flags.'

'YOU PROBABLY didn't hear that my local library won the Best Library of the Year Award,' says Dan Sutherland. 'They like to keep it quiet.'

'I KNOW people claim money talks,' says reader Bob Murphy. 'But all mine ever says is ta-ta.'

ANOTHER UNLIKELY story from reader Bob Arnold, who says:

'Since the factory demoted me to seatbelt tester I've been strapped for cash.'

'IF YOU get into an argument on a canal boat,' wonders reader Steve Doyle, 'should it be described as a 'bit of argy-bargy?'

PHILOSOPHICALLY MINDED reader Norrie Johnstone has decided to revise the profound sayings of the learned Chinese sage Confucius. He suggests:

'Man who lives in glass house should change clothes in basement.'

WE CONTINUE updating the wise sayings of Confucius, with a reader suggesting:

'Man who leaps off cliff jumps to conclusion.'

ANOTHER CONFUCIUS amendment. A reader suggests:

'Man who eats many prunes gets good run for money.'

FRUSTRATED READER Mandy Arnold says:

'I called the urology department of the hospital recently and the nurse asked me if I could hold.'

IN A rather silly mood, reader William Bowden asks us:

'What's brown and sticky?' The answer is, of course: 'A stick.'

CARD PLAYING reader David Liddell asks if we know what is the most popular bid in American bridge circles? It's '4 No Trump', of course.

10
DRAGONS, GREGORIAN MONKS AND THE ABIDING MYSTERY OF SHAMPOO

THE problem with many classic fairy tales is that they tend to celebrate rampant prejudice and bigotry.

You rarely get a story that has a positive take on dragons, for instance, who are always criticised because of their predilection for collecting vast amounts of treasure, which they pile up in a cave then sit upon.

This is invariably described as boorish behaviour. Yet surely we should commend dragons for their ability to prudently save their income, instead of becoming spendthrifts who fritter away wealth on nights out at the pub or phoning for pizza home-deliveries?

Another sign of bigotry in fairy tales is the terrible way Cinderella's stepsisters are mocked. These ambitious go-getters are merely looking for love, social advancement and a fun night out on the lash. Which is pretty much what all teenagers sign up for when they swagger off to Uni. Nowadays that's called an education.

In this chapter we try to balance out the bigotry by scrutinising the Cinderella tale and finding a flaw within the core narrative. We also show a certain amount of sympathy towards the dragon community.

For readers who feel they have progressed past fairy tales, we have some very grown-up stories about rehab and the abiding mysteries of shampoo ...

SYMPATHETIC READER Sarah Butler says:

 'Isn't it sad that dragons can never blow out their birthday candles?'

'SAY SOMETHING wise and profound and you will be remembered for all eternity,' says Mary Palmer from Langside, who adds: 'I heard that somewhere. I think it was what's-his-face who said it.'

CONFUSED READER Tom Bruce says:

 'If Cinderella's shoe was a perfect fit why did it fall off in the first place?'

SPIRITUALLY MINDED reader Tod Hobart says:
  'I always wanted to be a Gregorian monk, but I never got the chants.'

CONCERNED READER Derek Bruce asks:
  'What happens if you get addicted to rehab?'

RUMINATIVE READER Roger Lloyd asks:
  'Does anyone actually use Head & Shoulders to wash their shoulders?'

CURIOUS READER Clive Scott asks:
  'Do locksmiths qualify as key workers?'

'I'M IN a band called The Blankets,' revealed reader Charles Miller. 'We do covers.'

INSPIRED BY the above query, reader Craig McCall asks:

'Is a docker a quay worker?'

INQUISITIVE READER Peter Morton says:

'If I repeatedly made jokes about brooms, would friends start referring to my 'broom shtick'?'

IRRITATED MUSIC fan Alex Wilson says:

'I hate it when I'm singing along with a song on the radio and the artist gets the lyrics wrong.'

KEEN FISHERMAN Alan Doyle asks:

'Does every fish I catch and throw back go home with an alien abduction story?'

THOUGHTFUL READER Tony Drummond muses:
   'If psychic phonelines are genuine, why don't they call you?'

WE LIVE in a world where trust has almost entirely been eroded, sometimes even inside the home. With this in mind, a reader says:
   'Don't be worried about your smartphone and TV spying on you. Your vacuum cleaner has been gathering dirt on you for years.'

'I CAN tell people are judgemental just by looking at them,' says reader Charles Miller.

COVETOUS READER Mike Sharpe informs us he has saved stacks of old magazines in his loft.
   'Does this mean I've got issues?' he wonders.

FRUSTRATED READER Joe Knox recently waited four days for an electrician to call.

'Then I got word from the company that he wouldn't be coming as he had to self-insulate,' sighs Joe.

AN ARCHITECTURAL enquiry from reader Tom Beale who asks:

'Why is it called a building when it's already built?'

PERPLEXED READER Nigel Stewart phones to tell us he has lost his DVD of the movie *Gone in 60 Seconds*.

'It was here a minute ago,' he sighs.

A DUBIOUS money-making scheme from reader Jordan Nevill, who wonders:

'If I played poker with tarot cards would I win a fortune?'

HISTORICALLY MINDED reader Matt Hannah tells us:

'Before the crowbar was invented crows just drank at home.'

WITH ITS cheerful disposition a dog is often described as a man's best friend. Other pets are not always so affectionate, points out reader Marc Oliver, who says:

'I can never tell what my pet fish wants. Why does he have to be so koi?'

HELPFUL ADVICE from reader Derek Morgan:
 'Always wear a balaclava to bed. If you're robbed in the night they'll think you're part of the gang.'

OUR CORRESPONDENTS are often intrigued by the eccentricities of language. Arnold Garner says:
 'The word "queue" is ironic because it's just a "q" then a bunch of silent letters waiting in a line.'

THE THRILLING hobby of fishing reminds reader Tom Garner of the time he attempted to persuade his American wife they should take up the pursuit. To which she responded:
 'Fishing's a jerk on one end of a line waiting for a jerk on the other end of the line.'

INSPIRING WORDS from reader Martin Harris:

'To err is human. To blame it on someone else shows management potential.'

A SAD reminiscence from reader Pete Coe, who says:

'My father wasn't in the picture much as I was growing up. He was a portrait photographer.'

THOUGHT FOR the day from reader Robert Williams, who says:

'Whoever decided to call them dentures missed a great opportunity to invent the word "substitooths".'

WELL TRAVELLED reader Sam Fowler tells us Argentina has a surprisingly cold climate.

'It's bordering on Chile,' he explains.

SCAREDY-CAT READER Steven Burns is terrified of spiders:

'I was hoping to find an arachnophobia support group,' he says. 'But they don't appear to have a website.'

THE PERSON who invented anti-itch cream probably wasn't as clever as the developers of the coronavirus vaccine, concedes reader Keir MacLeod. Though he still believes they did an impressive job.

'After all, they had to start from scratch,' he explains.

CULINARY CONFUSION is supplied by Bob Miller from Airdrie, who asks:

'Do all vegetarian pasties have to be made in Quornwall?'

'MY DOG broke my mirror,' sighs Bob Miller from Airdrie. 'Guess that's forty-nine years bad luck.'

THOUGHTFUL READER Robert Chadwick says:

'Do you realise the word "incorrectly" is spelled "incorrectly" in every English dictionary?'

'THE USA has many spectacular vistas,' notes well-travelled reader Frank Fowler. 'The beauty of Mount Rushmore before the carvings was unpresidented,' he points out.

WE CONTINUE to bravely contemplate those questions other joke books are too fearful to address. Reader Sarah Fraser asks:

'If people from Holland and the Philippines marry, are their children Hollapinos?'

IN A similar vein, reader John Mulholland asks:

'Is Donald Trump's refusal to accept that he's been "unpresidented" unprecedented?'

STRUGGLING TO pick the ideal Christmas gift for a loved one? Reader Martin Rose suggests a broken drum's the very thing.

'It's an unbeatable present,' he says.

A SAD tale of a career in ruins from reader David Marshall, who writes:

'It's totally unfair that I was fired on my first day as a signwirter.'

A PROFOUND thought from reader Ken Evans, who says:

'Never ask directions from a starfish.'

???

11
AND FINALLY . . .
QUIZ TIME!

Okay, the fun and games are over, pal. Now it's time for the serious stuff. To make sure you've been paying attention, we've got a few final questions regarding everything you've just read. (You better not have been skimming. And hopefully you took notes as you went along.)

If you manage to get most of the following questions right . . . well done! You really are a bit of a joker.

And if you fail the test? Now you know exactly what it feels like to be one of those people who bought the smash hit record *Agadoo* by Black Lace, back in 1984.

That's right. The shame and the pain will never leave you.

1. THE PURPOSE OF THIS BOOK IS . . .

A. It can be slipped under a shoogly coffee table leg, thus allowing you to enjoy afternoon tea without fearing that your fondant fancies and sticky buns are going to be scattered on the carpet. (Which probably hasn't even been vacuumed. Seriously, get that Dyson out the cupboard – *now*.)

B. It will look mightily impressive when visitors spot it sitting on your spiffy bookcase. Now they'll think you're a bona fide scholar! (Though you'll have to buy a spiffy bookcase, first. Try 'Spiffy Bookcases R Us'. They're bound to have at least one in stock.)

C. It will give you oodles of laughs. (An 'oodle' isn't an up-to-date measurement, by the way. It was replaced in 1970 by the metric system.)

D. You can always turn it into a helicopter, if the jokes aren't to your liking.

2. THOUSANDS OF YEARS AGO, CAVEMAN HUMOUR TENDED TO . . .

A. Be dry and sophisticated, like a society play written by Noel Coward.

B. Involve lots of hefty clubs and sound effects that went: 'Boink!'

C. Be exceedingly unpopular with woolly mammoths, who on the whole had pessimistic dispositions and preferred watching tragedies rather than upbeat light entertainment.

D. Be almost indistinguishable to a Bob
Monkhouse gag from 1979.

3. THE CHICKEN WHO CROSSED THE ROAD IN THE FAMOUS JOKE WAS . . .

A. Actually, a duck in the original version of the gag. However, because the chicken had strong union representation in the joke world, she managed to force the duck out of the job. The duck hasn't worked since and hardly leaves its pond. It mostly spends its time watching daytime TV and eating cheese and onion Pringles straight from the tube. A tragic tale . . .

B. Probably called Myrtle.

C. Definitely called Myrtle.

D. Extremely athletic. It actually crossed the road using a pole vault, though for some reason that's seldom mentioned in the original joke.

4. THE PROBLEM WITH THE MET GALA IN NEW YORK IS THAT . . .

A. It's far too inclusive an event. Anyone can go, no matter your income bracket or your social standing. And if you want to turn up in a sweaty old tracksuit with a soup-stained T-shirt? Knock yourself out! It's not as though anyone is going to be judgemental.

B. It's not really held in New York. That's just a slick marketing ruse. It actually takes place, every year, in downtown Plockton.

C. Trick question. There is no problem. In fact, the Met Gala represents humanity's greatest triumph in bringing about social cohesion, harmony and equality since Kim Kardashian asked us all to 'Give Peace A Chance'. (Or was that John and Yoko? Darn. We'll have to Google it . . .)

D. It's so deliciously ridiculous an occasion that it makes most jokes seem dull and commonplace in comparison.

5. DRAGONS HOARD TREASURE IN THEIR CAVES BECAUSE . . .

A. Since the global financial crash of 2007-2008 they don't trust any of the major high street banks to look after their loot.

B. Caves can get rather chilly and damp as they don't have central heating. A heap of treasure makes an excellent draft excluder and helps keep dragons toasty-warm during the chilly winter months.

C. They are prudent creatures who scorn the idea of wasting their savings on pizza and beer.

D. It's the only hobby they have. Most of them would prefer to collect first editions of classic novels or old comics. Though this would be a tad dangerous, what with the fiery breath of your average dragon, and the inherent flammability of books and comics.

ANSWERS

1. C & D

2. B

3. B

4. D

5. C

C000258248

Cheating True Love: Sibusiso's Transformative Journey

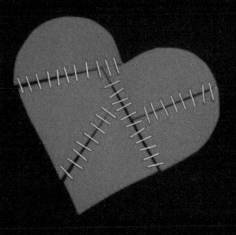

A novel by

Sibusiso Anthon Mkhwanazi

Cheating Hearts to True Love:
Sibusiso's Transformative Journey

While every precaution has been taken in the preparation of this book, the publisher assumes no responsibility for errors or omissions, or for damages resulting from the use of the information contained herein.

CHEATING HEARTS TO TRUE LOVE

First edition. December 1, 2023.

Copyright © 2023 Sibusiso Anthon Mkhwanazi.

ISBN: 979-8223086550

Written by Sibusiso Anthon Mkhwanazi.

Chapter 1: Introduction

In the vibrant city of Johannesburg, where the heartbeat of South Africa's urban life resonates, there lived a man named Sibusiso Mkhwanazi. Charismatic and successful, Sibusiso was a striking figure in the bustling metropolis. Tall and well-built, with a warm smile that could melt hearts, he had an aura that drew people towards him like moths to a flame. He was the kind of man who left an indelible mark wherever he went.

Sibusiso's success wasn't merely a result of his dashing good looks; he had an entrepreneurial spirit that drove him to establish his own tech startup, which quickly became a rising star in the industry. He possessed a sharp mind and a knack for innovation that was nothing short of impressive.

But beyond his professional achievements, Sibusiso was known for something else: his fervent belief in the power of love. From a young age, he had been captivated by the idea of finding his one true soulmate, someone with whom he could share the deepest corners of his heart and soul. He believed in the kind of love that transcended the ordinary and transformed lives.

Despite his many accomplishments, Sibusiso's romantic life had been a rollercoaster of emotions. His pursuit of love had led him down a path filled with heartbreak and disappointment. It seemed that every time he opened his heart to someone new, he was met with betrayal and deceit.

But he remained undeterred. Sibusiso Mkhwanazi was a man who refused to give up on love. He believed that somewhere out there, a woman existed who would restore his faith in the enduring power of love. Little did he know that his journey was about to take a remarkable turn, leading him to a woman named Nokulunga Cele, who would redefine everything he thought he knew about love and destiny.

The city of Johannesburg, with its towering skyscrapers and bustling streets, served as the backdrop to Sibusiso's quest for love. It was a city of contrasts, where the fast-paced corporate world clashed with the vibrant rhythms of its diverse communities. In this dynamic environment, love and relationships took on various forms, from passionate whirlwinds to heartbreaking betrayals.

Amidst the urban chaos, the theme of love and relationships painted a canvas of emotions that transcended borders and backgrounds. It was a theme woven into the very fabric of the city's existence. From the intimate cafés in Maboneng to the scenic beauty of Walter Sisulu Botanical Gardens, love stories unfolded against the tapestry of Johannesburg's rich culture.

As Sibusiso navigated the intricacies of the city's dating scene, he found himself drawn into a world where love was both elusive and enchanting. The theme of love was like a siren's song, luring him into the depths of his heart's desires, only to test his resolve and strength time and time again.

In this city, love was a complex dance, filled with twists and turns, joy and sorrow, trust and betrayal. It was a theme that explored the depths of human connection, the fragility of trust, and the resilience of the human spirit.

Sibusiso's journey would not only be a personal one but also a reflection of the universal human experience—our unyielding pursuit of love and the profound impact it has on our lives. In the midst of Johannesburg's chaos, he would learn that love could be both a source of pain and the most exquisite form of redemption. His quest for true love would become a story that resonated with anyone who had ever dared to dream of finding their soulmate amidst the complexities of modern relationships.

Chapter 2: Sibusiso's First Love

Sibusiso's journey through the labyrinth of love began during his college years when he met Thandiwe, a vivacious and enchanting young woman with a radiant smile that lit up any room. Their love story blossomed on the campus of the University of Johannesburg, against a backdrop of lectures, late-night study sessions, and dreams of the future.

Thandiwe was the kind of woman who captured Sibusiso's heart effortlessly. She had an infectious laughter that could turn a mundane day into an adventure. Their connection was immediate, and their love was all-consuming, as if fate had orchestrated their meeting.

As their relationship deepened, Sibusiso's world revolved around Thandiwe. He admired her intelligence, her passion for social justice, and the way she made him feel like the luckiest man alive. They often spent weekends exploring the city, holding hands as they strolled through the Johannesburg Botanical Garden, sharing dreams of building a future together.

However, as the months passed, a shadow began to creep into their love story. Sibusiso started noticing subtle changes in Thandiwe's behavior—late nights at the library, unanswered calls, and whispered phone conversations. His instincts told him that something was amiss, but he dismissed his doubts, unwilling to believe that the love he had found could be tainted by betrayal.

One fateful evening, as he surprised Thandiwe with a bouquet of her favorite flowers, he discovered the painful truth. The sound of hushed voices from her dorm room drew him closer, and he couldn't help but overhear a conversation that shattered his world. Thandiwe was confessing her love for another man, someone she had met at a charity event—a man named Jabulani.

Sibusiso's heart sank as he listened to their conversation, realizing that Thandiwe had been cheating on him for months. Tears welled up in his eyes, and he felt a crushing weight in his chest as he confronted her about the affair.

Their once-cherished love story had come crashing down, leaving Sibusiso with a profound sense of heartbreak and betrayal. It was a painful lesson that would forever shape his understanding of love, trust, and the complexities of human relationships. Thandiwe's infidelity marked the beginning of Sibusiso's tumultuous journey through the highs and lows of love, pushing him further down the path toward finding his true soulmate, Nokulunga Cele.

After his first heartbreak with Thandiwe, Sibusiso felt like he was carrying the weight of the world on his shoulders. The streets of Johannesburg, once bustling with the promise of love, had now become a cold and unfeeling place. He couldn't shake the memories of their love, the promises made under the city lights, and the bitter taste of betrayal that had shattered it all. With a heavy heart, he made the decision to leave Johannesburg behind, believing that the city was meant for business, not for matters of the heart. It was time for a fresh start, and the coastal city of Durban beckoned like a beacon of hope—a place where he could heal, rebuild, and perhaps, one day, find a love that would be truer and more enduring than any he had known before.

As he boarded the train to Durban, Sibusiso watched the city skyline of Johannesburg disappear in the distance. He knew that this journey was not just a physical one but a journey of the heart, a quest to rediscover the essence of love, trust, and resilience. Durban, with its warm sea breeze and the promise of new beginnings, held the key to his transformation—a place where he could rewrite the narrative of his love life and where the lessons of his past heartbreak would serve as guiding stars on his transformative voyage.

HERE'S AN OVERVIEW of chapters dedicated to each of Sibusiso's 15 Zulu girlfriends, focusing on different types of cheating experiences and the lessons learned:

Chapter 3: Nompumelelo's Deceit

Nompumelelo, a woman of grace and beauty, stepped into Sibusiso's life with an enchanting allure that was impossible to ignore. Their love story began in the heart of Durban, a city known for its golden beaches and vibrant culture. From the moment they met, there was an undeniable chemistry that seemed destined to ignite into a love that would conquer all.

Nompumelelo was an enigma of contradictions. Her captivating smile and charismatic personality drew Sibusiso in, making him feel like the luckiest man in the world. Together, they explored the city's bustling markets, savoring local delicacies and sharing dreams of a future filled with adventure.

Yet, beneath the surface of their seemingly perfect love story, a dark shadow lurked. Nompumelelo's infidelity, like a venomous serpent, slowly poisoned their relationship. Late nights at the office, secretive phone calls, and her growing distance left Sibusiso with a gnawing sense of unease.

As doubt and suspicion festered, Sibusiso couldn't ignore the signs any longer. He confronted Nompumelelo one fateful evening, his heart pounding with a mix of fear and desperation. What he discovered shattered his trust in love. Nompumelelo confessed to her infidelity, revealing that she had been seeing another man named Sizwe behind his back.

The revelation hit Sibusiso like a tidal wave, leaving him gasping for air in a sea of heartbreak and betrayal. Nompumelelo's deceit shook the very foundation of his belief in love, leaving behind scars that would take time to heal.

In the aftermath of their shattered romance, Sibusiso faced a profound inner struggle. He grappled with the torment of lost trust, the agony of betrayal, and the haunting question of whether he could ever truly love and trust again. Nompumelelo's infidelity had left a lasting mark on his heart, casting a shadow over his future relationships.

As Sibusiso moved forward on his journey, he carried with him the painful lesson that love could be a double-edged sword, capable of bringing both euphoria and agony. Nompumelelo's deceit had forever altered the course of his quest for true love, instilling in him a newfound wariness and a yearning for a love that would be as honest and genuine as he had always hoped it could be.

Indeed, Sibusiso's painful experience with Nompumelelo taught him invaluable lessons about the importance of communication and trust in any relationship. This betrayal forced him to confront the following key lessons:

1. **Open and Honest Communication:** Sibusiso realized that keeping doubts, suspicions, and concerns hidden can be detrimental to a relationship. He understood that open and honest communication is the foundation of trust. In the future, he vowed to be more forthcoming with his feelings and to encourage his partners to do the same, fostering an environment where issues could be discussed and resolved openly.

2. **The Fragility of Trust:** Nompumelelo's infidelity showed Sibusiso just how fragile trust can be. He learned that trust is a cornerstone of love, and once it's broken, it can be incredibly challenging to rebuild. This experience left him more cautious about giving his trust too readily and reinforced the importance of being with someone who values and respects that trust.

3. Self-Worth and Boundaries: Sibusiso realized that he deserved to be with someone who honored their commitment to the relationship. Nompumelelo's actions taught him the importance of setting clear boundaries and recognizing his own self-worth. He resolved never to compromise on his values and standards in future relationships.

4. Healing and Self-Growth: While the pain of Nompumelelo's betrayal was intense, it also spurred Sibusiso on a journey of self-discovery and healing. He learned that healing takes time, and it's essential to give oneself the space and grace to recover from heartbreak. This experience made him stronger and more resilient.

As Sibusiso continued his quest for love, these lessons would serve as guiding principles, helping him navigate the complexities of future relationships with a deeper understanding of the importance of communication and trust.

Chapter 4: Sibongile's Hidden Secrets

S ibongile, a woman of elegance and allure, entered Sibusiso's life like a whirlwind. Their love story unfolded against the backdrop of Durban's enchanting beaches and lively nightlife, painting a picture of passion and promise. Sibongile had an air of mystery about her, an enigmatic quality that intrigued Sibusiso from the start.

Their connection was intense and immediate. Sibongile's sharp wit and magnetic charm drew Sibusiso in, making him feel like he was living in a dream. They reveled in exploring the city's culinary delights, sipping cocktails by the sea, and dreaming of a future filled with adventure and excitement.

Yet, beneath Sibongile's captivating exterior lay a labyrinth of secrets and half-truths. She was evasive about her past, often changing the subject when questioned about her family and upbringing. Sibusiso couldn't ignore the nagging feeling that there was more to Sibongile than met the eye.

As their relationship deepened, so did Sibusiso's curiosity. He felt compelled to uncover the truth about Sibongile's past, sensing that her hidden secrets were a ticking time bomb that threatened to destroy the trust they had built. Late one evening, after sharing an intimate dinner, he broached the subject with caution, urging Sibongile to open up about her past.

What he discovered would send shockwaves through their relationship. Sibongile confessed to a web of lies and half-truths, revealing that her mysterious past was filled with deception and secrets.

Her true identity and background were vastly different from what she had initially portrayed.

Sibongile's hidden secrets threatened to shatter the trust that had been the foundation of their love story. Sibusiso, torn between his feelings for her and the realization that their relationship was built on a foundation of lies, faced a heart-wrenching decision. Would he be able to forgive and rebuild, or would the weight of Sibongile's deception prove too much to bear?

In the wake of this revelation, Sibusiso grappled with the painful truth that love, while intoxicating and alluring, could also be a veil that concealed the darkness of hidden secrets. His journey to find true love became more complex, and he questioned whether he could ever truly know and trust someone again. Sibongile's hidden secrets had cast a shadow over his pursuit of love, leaving him with a deeper understanding of the complexities of human relationships and the fragility of trust.

In the aftermath of his tumultuous relationship with Sibongile, Sibusiso confronted a series of painful but invaluable lessons that would guide him in his quest for genuine love. Sibongile's hidden secrets taught him, above all else, the profound importance of honesty and openness in a relationship.

1. **The Fragility of Deception:** Sibongile's web of lies and half-truths revealed to Sibusiso just how fragile trust in a relationship could be. Her deception had threatened to shatter the bond they had built, demonstrating that trust, once broken, could be difficult to mend.

2. **Honesty as a Foundation:** Sibusiso came to understand that honesty is the cornerstone of any meaningful relationship. Sibongile's hidden secrets had eroded the trust they had cultivated, highlighting that genuine connections are built on a foundation of truth.

3. **The Value of Vulnerability:** Sibongile's unwillingness to be open about her past showed Sibusiso the significance of vulnerability in a relationship. He learned that true intimacy and connection require both

partners to share their authentic selves, including their pasts and insecurities.

4. Choosing Honesty over Illusion: Sibusiso realized that he wanted a love that was based on authenticity, not illusion. Sibongile's hidden secrets had created a façade that ultimately crumbled. He resolved to seek partners who were willing to be transparent and share their true selves, even if it meant revealing imperfections.

5. A Commitment to Truth: Sibusiso made a personal commitment to always be honest and open in his future relationships. He understood that fostering trust required not only truthfulness but also the willingness to listen and empathize with a partner's truths, no matter how challenging they might be.

As Sibusiso continued his journey, these lessons about the value of honesty and openness would serve as guiding principles, helping him navigate the complexities of love and relationships with a newfound appreciation for the importance of truth in building lasting connections.

Chapter 5: Thandeka's Temptation

Thandeka, a vibrant and spirited woman, entered Sibusiso's life like a burst of energy. Their love story unfolded in the vibrant cityscape of Durban, where the sun-kissed beaches and lively streets provided the backdrop to their passionate romance. Thandeka had a magnetic charisma that drew Sibusiso in from the very beginning.

Their connection was undeniable, and their relationship blossomed quickly. Thandeka's vivacious personality and love for adventure filled Sibusiso's life with excitement. They explored the city's culinary delights, danced to the rhythms of live music at jazz clubs, and dreamed of a future filled with spontaneity and passion.

However, beneath the surface of their intense love, a troubling pattern began to emerge. Thandeka's wandering eye and flirtatious nature led to temptation and betrayal. Sibusiso couldn't help but notice how her attention seemed to wander, how her eyes would linger a moment too long on other men, and how innocent conversations often took on a more flirtatious tone.

As doubt and insecurity gnawed at him, Sibusiso tried to rationalize Thandeka's behavior, convincing himself that it was harmless. But deep down, he knew that something was amiss. One evening, after a particularly heated argument about her interactions with other men, Thandeka confessed to her infidelity.

Her confession was a gut-wrenching blow to Sibusiso's heart. The woman he had loved so intensely had given in to temptation, betraying the trust they had built. The pain of her betrayal was excruciating, leaving him grappling with questions of whether their love could ever be the same again.

In the wake of Thandeka's betrayal, Sibusiso faced a heart-wrenching choice. He had to decide whether he could forgive her and rebuild their relationship or whether the scars of her infidelity ran too deep to heal.

SIBUSISO'S PAINFUL experience with Thandeka's temptation and betrayal taught him several crucial lessons:

1. **The Fragility of Temptation:** He came to understand the fragility of human willpower and the allure of temptation. Thandeka's wandering eye demonstrated that even the strongest relationships could be tested when faced with external temptations.

2. **The Importance of Boundaries:** Sibusiso realized the necessity of setting clear boundaries in a relationship. He learned that it's vital for both partners to respect these boundaries to maintain trust and fidelity.

3. **The Complex Nature of Forgiveness:** Sibusiso grappled with the complexity of forgiveness and the depth of emotional wounds caused by betrayal. He understood that forgiveness was a personal choice and that healing could take time.

4. **Communication and Rebuilding Trust:** Sibusiso recognized that rebuilding trust after betrayal required open and honest communication. He learned that it was essential for both partners to address the underlying issues that contributed to the infidelity.

As Sibusiso continued his journey to find true love, these lessons about temptation and betrayal would shape his approach to future relationships, emphasizing the importance of trust, communication, and fidelity in building lasting and meaningful connections.

Chapter 6: Nomvula's Confession

Nomvula, a woman with a mysterious aura and a smile that could brighten the darkest of days, became the next chapter in Sibusiso's quest for love. Their love story unfolded against the backdrop of Durban's scenic beauty, where the warm breeze off the Indian Ocean seemed to carry promises of everlasting happiness.

Nomvula was a woman of grace and charm, and her presence in Sibusiso's life was both captivating and comforting. They explored the city's hidden gems, shared laughter over street food, and whispered dreams of a future filled with love and adventure.

Yet, behind the façade of their seemingly perfect love story, a storm brewed in the shadows. Nomvula carried a hidden secret, one she had kept locked away deep within her heart. As their relationship deepened, she felt the weight of her secret pressing down on her.

One evening, with tears in her eyes and a trembling voice, Nomvula finally confessed her hidden truth to Sibusiso. Her secret was a revelation that shook the very foundation of their love, testing the depths of their connection and the strength of their commitment.

Sibusiso, shocked and hurt by the truth, faced a choice: to turn away from Nomvula in anger and disappointment, or to embrace her, flaws and all, in the hope of salvaging the love they had built.

This chapter in Sibusiso's journey would challenge his understanding of love and forgiveness, leaving him with lessons that would shape his future relationships and his quest for a love that transcended secrets and imperfections.

NOMVULA'S HEART-WRENCHING confession marked a pivotal moment in Sibusiso's journey, teaching him profound lessons about forgiveness and the value of second chances in matters of the heart.

1. **The Power of Forgiveness:** Nomvula's confession illuminated the incredible power of forgiveness. Sibusiso realized that forgiveness was not merely a gift to be given to others but also a gift to himself. It allowed him to release the burden of anger and resentment, freeing his heart from the pain of betrayal.

2. **The Complexity of Human Imperfection:** Nomvula's hidden secret reminded Sibusiso that no one was without flaws or imperfections. He learned that understanding and accepting these imperfections were essential components of love. It was through forgiveness that he embraced the complexity of human nature.

3. **The Strength of Second Chances:** Sibusiso's decision to give Nomvula a second chance illustrated his belief in the strength of their love. He understood that relationships could endure hardships and emerge stronger when both partners were willing to work through their issues and grow together.

4. **The Healing Process:** Sibusiso's journey of forgiveness became a part of his healing process. It taught him that healing required not only time but also the willingness to let go of past pain and embrace the possibility of a better future.

5. **The Beauty of Vulnerability:** Through Nomvula's confession, Sibusiso discovered the beauty of vulnerability in a relationship. He recognized that when partners were open and honest with each other, even in the face of difficult truths, it could strengthen their bond and create a deeper sense of intimacy.

As Sibusiso continued his quest for love, the lessons learned from his experience with Nomvula's confession would serve as a reminder of the transformative power of forgiveness and the value of second chances. He was now better equipped to navigate the complexities of love, understanding that, at its core, love was about embracing imperfections and choosing forgiveness as a path to lasting happiness.

Chapter 7: Thembi's Betrayal

Thembi, a woman of elegance and sophistication, entered Sibusiso's life like a breath of fresh air. Their love story unfolded against the backdrop of Durban's enchanting evenings, where the city lights danced upon the ocean waves, creating a scene that seemed straight out of a fairy tale.

Thembi's intelligence and poise were magnetic, drawing Sibusiso into a whirlwind romance filled with intellectual conversations, fine dining, and dreams of a future filled with success and happiness. They shared laughter, dreams, and a deep sense of connection that seemed unbreakable.

However, beneath the surface of their seemingly perfect love story, a storm brewed. Thembi's betrayal was about to shock Sibusiso to the core, testing the very foundations of trust and love upon which their relationship was built.

One evening, as they were preparing for a romantic dinner, Thembi's phone rang with an incoming call. Sibusiso, who had always trusted her completely, thought nothing of it. But as he moved closer to help set the table, he caught a glimpse of the caller's name—Mandla.

The name struck a chord of familiarity in Sibusiso's mind. Mandla was a name he had heard before, and the pieces of a painful puzzle began to fall into place. The sinking feeling in his gut grew stronger as Thembi hesitated to answer the call.

With trembling hands and a heart pounding with dread, Sibusiso confronted Thembi about the call. What he discovered shattered his trust in love once again—Thembi had been in a secret relationship with Mandla, a man from her past, even while professing her love for Sibusiso.

The revelation hit Sibusiso like a tidal wave, leaving him gasping for breath in a sea of heartbreak and betrayal. The woman he had loved and trusted implicitly had been living a double life, concealing her affair with Mandla from him.

In the aftermath of Thembi's shocking betrayal, Sibusiso faced a profound sense of disillusionment. He questioned the very nature of love and trust, wondering if he would ever be able to find a love that was genuine and true.

This chapter in Sibusiso's journey would force him to confront the depths of deception and the pain of betrayal, leaving him with wounds that would take time to heal. Yet, it would also teach him lessons about resilience and the enduring quest for a love that was worth the pain and heartache.

Thembi's shocking betrayal plunged Sibusiso into the depths of pain and despair, but it also imparted profound lessons about the resilience of the human spirit and the strength to move forward after betrayal.

1. **Understanding the Pain of Betrayal:** Thembi's betrayal laid bare the excruciating pain that comes with being betrayed by someone you love and trust. Sibusiso experienced firsthand the emotional turmoil, heartache, and disillusionment that betrayal can bring. It allowed him to empathize with the struggles of others who had faced similar betrayals.

2. **The Complexity of Human Nature:** Thembi's double life underscored the complexity of human nature. Sibusiso came to recognize that people could harbor hidden desires and secrets that might lead them down a path of betrayal, even when they genuinely cared for their partner. It was a reminder that no one was entirely predictable or free from vulnerabilities.

3. **The Power of Resilience:** Sibusiso discovered his own resilience in the face of heartbreak. He realized that, even after enduring the pain of betrayal, he possessed the strength to move forward and rebuild his

ife. This newfound resilience became a source of empowerment for him, showing him that he could overcome even the most challenging setbacks.

4. **The Importance of Self-Care:** After Thembi's betrayal, Sibusiso learned the importance of self-care and self-compassion. He understood that healing required tending to his own well-being and allowing himself the time and space to recover from the emotional wounds inflicted by betrayal.

5. **A Renewed Quest for Authentic Love:** This experience renewed Sibusiso's determination to find a love that was authentic and true. He realized that while betrayal could leave deep scars, it didn't mean he should give up on the quest for genuine love. It motivated him to continue seeking a relationship built on trust and honesty.

As Sibusiso continued his journey, these lessons about the pain of betrayal and the strength to move on would serve as a source of resilience and determination. He understood that life's challenges, including heartbreak, could be transformative experiences that ultimately guided him toward a deeper understanding of love and the quest for a love that would endure.

Chapter 8: Siphokazi's Secret Life

Siphokazi, a woman of mystery and allure, stepped into Sibusiso's life like a captivating enigma. Their love story unfolded against the backdrop of Durban's enchanting evenings, where the city's lights danced upon the ocean waves, promising a future filled with romance and excitement.

Siphokazi possessed an air of sophistication that drew Sibusiso in from the very beginning. Her intelligence, wit, and charming smile made him feel like he had met someone truly extraordinary. Together, they explored the city's cultural treasures, indulged in fine dining, and dreamed of a life brimming with adventure and success.

However, beneath the surface of their seemingly perfect love story, a dark secret was concealed. Siphokazi was living a double life, and the truth about her hidden identity was about to shatter their relationship.

One evening, as they were sharing a quiet dinner at their favorite restaurant, Siphokazi received an unexpected message on her phone. Sibusiso, who had always trusted her implicitly, thought nothing of it at first. But the tone of her voice and the urgency with which she excused herself raised his suspicions.

With a heavy heart and a sense of foreboding, Sibusiso decided to investigate further. He unlocked Siphokazi's phone to find answers to the questions that had begun to plague his mind. What he discovered in that moment was a devastating revelation—Siphokazi had been leading a secret life, concealing her true identity and the existence of a husband and children from Sibusiso.

The truth struck Sibusiso like a bolt of lightning, leaving him paralyzed with shock and disbelief. The woman he had loved so deeply had kept a profound secret, and their love was built on a foundation of deception.

In the aftermath of Siphokazi's shocking revelation, Sibusiso faced a harrowing decision. He had to grapple with the heart-wrenching choice of whether to continue a relationship marred by deception or to walk away, seeking a love that was founded on honesty and trust.

This chapter in Sibusiso's journey would force him to confront the depths of deceit and the pain of shattered trust, leaving him with wounds that would take time to heal. Yet, it would also serve as a stark reminder of the importance of authenticity and transparency in the pursuit of genuine love.

Siphokazi's double life and the heart-wrenching betrayal it entailed left Sibusiso with profound lessons about the value of authenticity and the significance of self-discovery in the pursuit of love.

1. **The Importance of Authenticity:** Sibusiso's painful experience with Siphokazi's deception underscored the crucial role of authenticity in any meaningful relationship. He realized that genuine love could only thrive when both partners were honest and open about their true selves. Authenticity became a non-negotiable principle in his future search for love.

2. **The Destructive Nature of Deception:** Siphokazi's double life had destructive consequences, causing immense pain and suffering. Sibusiso learned that deceit could erode the trust and intimacy that form the foundation of a healthy relationship. He vowed never to tolerate dishonesty in future relationships.

3. **The Journey of Self-Discovery:** Sibusiso's encounter with Siphokazi prompted him to embark on a journey of self-discovery. He realized that understanding one's own values, desires, and boundaries was essential to finding a compatible partner. He became more attuned

to his own needs and aspirations, using this self-awareness as a guide in his pursuit of love.

4. **Seeking Genuine Connections:** Sibusiso's experience with Siphokazi deepened his desire for authentic connections. He recognized that he wanted a love that was built on shared values and mutual respect, rather than superficial appearances or hidden agendas.

5. **The Healing Power of Honesty:** In the aftermath of Siphokazi's betrayal, Sibusiso found solace in the healing power of honesty and open communication. He realized that discussing his feelings and experiences with trusted friends and family helped him process the pain and move forward.

As Sibusiso continued his quest for love, these lessons about the value of authenticity and self-discovery would serve as guiding principles. He understood that the pursuit of genuine love required not only finding the right partner but also being the right partner—someone who valued authenticity, honesty, and the transformative power of self-discovery.

Chapter 9: Nokukhanya's Lies

Nokukhanya, a woman of beauty and grace, entered Sibusiso's life like a ray of sunshine. Their love story unfolded against the backdrop of Durban's picturesque sunsets, promising a future filled with warmth and happiness.

Nokukhanya's kindness and infectious laughter drew Sibusiso in, making him feel like he had found a love that was pure and genuine. Together, they explored the city's cultural treasures, shared dreams of travel, and reveled in the simple pleasures of life.

Yet, beneath the surface of their seemingly perfect love story, a shadow loomed. Nokukhanya's web of lies was about to strain their relationship to the breaking point.

As their relationship deepened, Sibusiso began to notice inconsistencies in Nokukhanya's stories. Small white lies and half-truths piled up, creating a growing sense of unease within him. He couldn't ignore the nagging feeling that something was amiss.

One evening, after an argument about her secrecy and evasiveness, Nokukhanya finally confessed to her lies. What she revealed was a complex tapestry of deception, concealing not only her true past but also a series of financial troubles and debts that threatened to engulf their future.

Sibusiso's trust in love was once again shaken to its core. The woman he had loved so deeply had woven a web of lies that threatened to unravel their relationship. He faced a heart-wrenching decision—to forgive and help Nokukhanya overcome her difficulties or to walk away, seeking a love founded on honesty and trust.

This chapter in Sibusiso's journey would test his capacity for forgiveness and challenge his belief in the possibility of love that transcended the weight of deception. It would leave him with lessons about the complexities of human nature and the enduring quest for a love that was built on truth and understanding.

Nokukhanya's web of lies and the strain it put on their relationship left Sibusiso with crucial lessons about the paramount importance of truth and trust in any meaningful connection.

1. **The Foundation of Trust:** Sibusiso's experience with Nokukhanya reinforced the belief that trust was the cornerstone of a healthy and enduring relationship. He understood that without trust, a partnership was destined to crumble under the weight of deception.

2. **The Erosion of Deception:** Nokukhanya's lies illustrated the destructive nature of deception. Sibusiso witnessed how even seemingly harmless white lies could escalate into a complex web of untruths, eroding the authenticity and intimacy of their relationship.

3. **The Value of Transparency:** Sibusiso learned the value of transparency and open communication. He recognized that it was essential for both partners to be honest about their pasts, their feelings, and their challenges. Transparency was the antidote to the poison of secrecy.

4. **The Healing Power of Forgiveness:** Sibusiso's choice to forgive Nokukhanya demonstrated his belief in the possibility of redemption and growth, even after deception. He understood that forgiveness could be a catalyst for healing and transformation, for both individuals and their relationship.

5. **Seeking Honesty and Authenticity:** Nokukhanya's lies prompted Sibusiso to seek partners who valued honesty and authenticity as much as he did. He resolved to be with someone who shared his commitment to openness and trust.

As Sibusiso continued his quest for love, these lessons about the importance of truth and trust would serve as guiding principles. He had experienced firsthand the consequences of deception and the pain it would inflict on a relationship. With a deeper understanding of the value of honesty and transparency, he hoped to find a love that was not only genuine but also enduring.

Chapter 10: Zinhle's Temptation

Zinhle, a vivacious and magnetic woman, entered Sibusiso's life like a whirlwind of excitement. Their love story continued to unfold against the backdrop of Durban's captivating scenery, where each sunset painted a promise of passion and adventure.

Zinhle's zest for life and her infectious laughter brought joy to Sibusiso's world. They shared dreams of exploring far-off destinations, dancing under the stars, and embracing the thrill of life's adventures together.

However, beneath the surface of their seemingly perfect love story, a familiar pattern began to emerge. Zinhle's wandering heart and flirtatious nature led to temptation and heartbreak once again. Sibusiso couldn't ignore the signs—the lingering gazes at other men, the late nights out with friends, and the unexplained absences that left him feeling insecure.

Doubt and insecurity gnawed at Sibusiso as he tried to rationalize Zinhle's behavior. But deep down, he knew that something was amiss. One fateful evening, after an argument about her increasing distance and distracted demeanor, Zinhle finally confessed to her infidelity.

The revelation was a devastating blow to Sibusiso's heart. The woman he had loved with all his heart had given in to temptation, betraying the trust they had built together. The pain of her betrayal was overwhelming, leaving him to grapple with questions of whether their love could ever be the same again.

In the wake of Zinhle's betrayal, Sibusiso faced another heart-wrenching decision. He had to determine whether he could forgive her and rebuild their relationship or whether the wounds of her infidelity were too deep to heal.

This chapter in Sibusiso's journey would force him to confront the recurring theme of temptation and betrayal, leaving him with a profound understanding of the complexities of human nature and the challenges of trust and fidelity in love.

Zinhle's temptation and subsequent betrayal brought Sibusiso face to face with the fragile nature of relationships, imparting valuable lessons about love and trust.

1. **The Fragility of Trust:** Zinhle's infidelity underscored just how fragile trust could be in a relationship. Sibusiso learned that trust was not only difficult to build but also remarkably easy to shatter. This experience deepened his understanding of the importance of trust as a foundation for lasting love.

2. **The Complexities of Temptation:** Sibusiso witnessed the complexities of human temptation and desire. He recognized that even the strongest relationships could be tested when faced with external temptations. This awareness made him more empathetic to the struggles that individuals might encounter within the confines of monogamous commitments.

3. **The Emotional Toll of Betrayal:** Zinhle's betrayal inflicted an emotional toll that was difficult to bear. Sibusiso experienced the depths of pain and heartbreak that often accompany betrayal, teaching him that the wounds of infidelity could take time to heal.

4. **The Need for Open Communication:** Sibusiso came to understand the importance of open and honest communication in addressing relationship challenges. He realized that issues left unspoken could fester and lead to the erosion of trust. Open conversations were essential for resolving conflicts and rebuilding a sense of security.

5. **The Resilience of the Human Spirit:** Despite the pain of betrayal, Sibusiso discovered the resilience of the human spirit. He recognized his own capacity to endure hardships and emerge stronger.

This newfound resilience became a source of strength as he navigated the complexities of love.

As Sibusiso continued his quest for love, these lessons about the fragility of relationships would serve as a constant reminder of the need for trust, open communication, and a deep commitment to nurturing and protecting the love he sought. He had learned that love, while beautiful, could also be incredibly delicate, and it was up to both partners to safeguard it with care and understanding.

Chapter 11: Nomfundo's Regret

Nomfundo, a woman with a mysterious past and a heart marked by regret, became the next chapter in Sibusiso's quest for love. Their love story unfolded against the backdrop of Durban's enchanting evenings, where the city's lights reflected off the tranquil ocean waves, promising a future filled with warmth and companionship.

Nomfundo's quiet demeanor and introspective nature intrigued Sibusiso from the very beginning. She carried a sense of mystery about her, and he felt drawn to unravel the layers of her past. Together, they explored the city's art galleries, shared stories of their dreams and aspirations, and reveled in the beauty of quiet moments spent in each other's company.

However, as their relationship deepened, Sibusiso began to sense a shadow lurking in Nomfundo's eyes—a shadow of past regrets and unspoken sorrow. It was as though her past weighed heavily on her heart, casting a pall over their love.

One evening, as they sat on the balcony, sipping tea and watching the stars, Nomfundo finally opened up about the regrets that had haunted her for years. She shared stories of past decisions and choices that had left her with a profound sense of remorse.

Nomfundo's confessions were a bittersweet revelation, one that touched Sibusiso's heart deeply. Her regrets weighed on their relationship, testing their love in ways he had never imagined. He faced a challenging decision—to offer understanding, support, and a chance for healing or to walk away in the face of her past mistakes.

This chapter in Sibusiso's journey would lead him to confront the complexities of human regrets and the power of compassion and empathy in the quest for lasting love. It would leave him with lessons about the importance of understanding and forgiveness as he sought to navigate the intricacies of a relationship marked by past choices and the hope for redemption.

Nomfundo's past regrets and their impact on their relationship taught Sibusiso profound lessons about the transformative power of forgiveness and the importance of empathy in matters of the heart.

1. **The Healing Power of Forgiveness:** Sibusiso's willingness to forgive Nomfundo for her past mistakes demonstrated the incredible healing power of forgiveness. He learned that forgiveness was not only a gift to the person seeking redemption but also a gift to himself. It allowed him to release judgment and resentment, creating space for healing and growth.

2. **The Complexity of Human Regrets:** Nomfundo's regrets showed Sibusiso the depth and complexity of human regrets. He realized that everyone carried their own burdens of past mistakes and decisions. This awareness made him more empathetic toward others and less judgmental of imperfections.

3. **The Value of Vulnerability:** Through Nomfundo's confessions, Sibusiso discovered the value of vulnerability in a relationship. He understood that when partners were open and honest about their past regrets, it could strengthen their bond and create a deeper sense of intimacy.

4. **The Importance of Compassion:** Sibusiso's decision to offer understanding and support to Nomfundo emphasized the importance of compassion in love. He recognized that showing compassion and empathy toward a partner's regrets could be a source of healing and growth for both individuals.

5. **A Commitment to Second Chances:** Sibusiso's experience with Nomfundo reinforced his belief in the possibility of second chances in

ove. He understood that people could learn from their mistakes and make positive changes in their lives, and that love had the capacity to be a source of redemption.

As Sibusiso continued his quest for love, these lessons about forgiveness and empathy would guide him in his pursuit of meaningful and enduring relationships. He had learned that love, when infused with understanding and forgiveness, had the power to heal wounds and create a future that was marked by hope and redemption.

Chapter 12: Nonhlanhla's Infidelity

Nonhlanhla, a woman with a magnetic personality and a zest for life, entered Sibusiso's world like a burst of energy. Their love story continued to unfold in the vibrant city of Durban, where the bustling streets and rhythmic music provided the backdrop to their passionate romance.

Nonhlanhla's charisma and free spirit drew Sibusiso in from the very beginning. Their love was an exhilarating journey filled with spontaneous adventures, late-night dancing, and dreams of a future filled with joy and excitement.

However, beneath the surface of their seemingly perfect love story, a cloud of suspicion began to form. Nonhlanhla's erratic behavior, secretive phone calls, and frequent absences aroused Sibusiso's fears of infidelity.

As doubt and insecurity gnawed at him, Sibusiso tried to ignore the signs, convincing himself that his suspicions were unfounded. But one fateful evening, as he unexpectedly walked into a scene he had never anticipated, the truth came crashing down on him—Nonhlanhla had been unfaithful.

The revelation was a devastating blow to Sibusiso's heart. The woman he had loved with all his soul had betrayed their trust, leaving him grappling with questions of whether love was nothing more than a fragile illusion.

In the aftermath of Nonhlanhla's infidelity, Sibusiso faced a profound crisis of faith in love. He questioned whether true love was attainable or if it was simply an idealized fantasy.

This chapter in Sibusiso's journey would test the very essence of his belief in love, leaving him with lessons about the complexities of human desires and the fragility of trust. It would force him to confront the painful reality of infidelity and the challenges of rebuilding a love that had been shattered.

NONHLANHLA'S INFIDELITY and its aftermath exposed Sibusiso to the intricate and often bewildering complexity of human emotions, imparting invaluable lessons about the multifaceted nature of love and trust.

1. **The Complexity of Desires:** Nonhlanhla's infidelity illuminated the complexity of human desires and needs. Sibusiso came to realize that individuals could be driven by a multitude of emotions and impulses, and that these complexities often played a significant role in their actions.

2. **The Fragility of Trust:** Nonhlanhla's betrayal underscored just how fragile trust could be. Sibusiso learned that trust, once broken, was not easily mended, and it required a significant amount of effort and time to rebuild.

3. **The Pain of Heartbreak:** Sibusiso experienced firsthand the excruciating pain of heartbreak caused by infidelity. He understood that heartbreak was not only an emotional ordeal but also a physical one, manifesting as a deep ache in the chest.

4. **The Challenge of Forgiveness:** Sibusiso grappled with the challenge of forgiveness in the wake of Nonhlanhla's infidelity. He recognized that forgiving someone who had betrayed his trust was an arduous journey that required introspection and a willingness to let go of anger and resentment.

5. **The Quest for Authentic Love:** Nonhlanhla's betrayal renewed Sibusiso's quest for authentic love. He understood that the pursuit of genuine love was fraught with complexities, but it was a journey worth

undertaking. He was determined to find a love that transcended the pain of infidelity and betrayal.

As Sibusiso continued his journey, these lessons about the complexity of human emotions would serve as a reminder of the intricacies that often define relationships. He had learned that love was not a simple or straightforward path; it was a journey marked by twists and turns, highs and lows, and the ever-present possibility of redemption and renewal.

Chapter 13: Khethiwe's Ultimatum

Khethiwe, a woman with a strong sense of purpose and determination, entered Sibusiso's life like a force of nature. Their love story continued to unfold against the backdrop of Durban's dynamic energy, where the city's aspirations mirrored their own dreams of a shared future filled with ambition and success.

Khethiwe's ambition and drive were qualities that both attracted and challenged Sibusiso. Their love was marked by spirited debates, mutual support in their respective endeavors, and dreams of achieving greatness side by side.

However, beneath the surface of their seemingly perfect love story, a storm began to brew. Khethiwe's relentless pursuit of her career and personal goals led her to issue an ultimatum—Sibusiso had to choose between his own dreams and aspirations and their relationship.

The ultimatum was a painful revelation for Sibusiso. The woman he loved deeply was now asking him to make an agonizing choice, one that felt like a betrayal of their shared dreams and a test of his commitment to their love.

As he grappled with Khethiwe's ultimatum, Sibusiso faced a heart-wrenching decision—whether to follow his own ambitions and aspirations or to sacrifice them for the sake of their love. This chapter in his journey would challenge the very essence of his commitment to love and the sacrifices that often came with it, leaving him with profound lessons about the complexities of balancing personal goals with the demands of a relationship.

KHETHIWE'S ULTIMATUM forced Sibusiso to confront the delicate balance between personal ambition and commitment to love, ultimately imparting crucial lessons about the value of compromise and unwavering commitment.

1. **The Power of Compromise:** Sibusiso learned that love often required compromise. Khethiwe's ultimatum made him realize that in a relationship, both partners had to make sacrifices and adjust their individual goals to create a harmonious and fulfilling partnership.

2. **The Challenge of Prioritization:** Khethiwe's demand to choose between career aspirations and their relationship highlighted the challenge of prioritization. Sibusiso understood that balancing personal ambitions with the demands of love required thoughtful consideration and careful decision-making.

3. **The Strength of Commitment:** Sibusiso's determination to find a middle ground in the face of Khethiwe's ultimatum showcased the strength of his commitment to their love. He recognized that true commitment meant not only staying together during the easy times but also navigating the difficult moments with dedication and resilience.

4. **The Need for Communication:** This experience reinforced the importance of open and honest communication in a relationship. Sibusiso understood that he and Khethiwe needed to discuss their goals and aspirations openly to find common ground and create a future that satisfied both their dreams.

5. **Seeking Mutual Fulfillment:** Sibusiso's decision to seek a compromise rather than choose one path over the other emphasized his belief in the possibility of mutual fulfillment. He realized that a relationship could thrive when both partners felt supported in their individual pursuits while also nurturing their love.

As Sibusiso continued his quest for love, these lessons about compromise and commitment would serve as guiding principles. He had learned that love was not only about passion and romance but also about he willingness to make sacrifices and work together to create a future hat honored both partners' aspirations and dreams.

Chapter 14: Phindile's Disappearance

Phindile, a woman with an air of mystery and an enigmatic charm, entered Sibusiso's life like a riddle waiting to be solved. Their love story continued to unfold against the backdrop of Durban's intriguing secrets, where the city's hidden corners mirrored the mysteries of their own hearts.

Phindile's captivating presence and her ability to keep him guessing drew Sibusiso in from the very beginning. Their love was an enigmatic journey filled with unexpected surprises, late-night adventures, and dreams of a future filled with intrigue and passion.

However, beneath the surface of their seemingly perfect love story, a sense of uncertainty loomed. Phindile's life was shrouded in secrets, and her frequent disappearances without explanation left Sibusiso with unanswered questions.

As he searched for clues and sought to understand the enigma that was Phindile, he uncovered a trail of secrets that led to her mysterious past. Yet, one day, Phindile disappeared without a trace, leaving Sibusiso to grapple with a sense of loss and confusion.

Her disappearance was a haunting riddle that left him with more questions than answers. Sibusiso faced the daunting challenge of unraveling the mystery of Phindile's life and understanding the reasons behind her sudden departure.

This chapter in Sibusiso's journey would force him to confront the enigmatic nature of love and the complexities of human relationships. It would leave him with lessons about the importance of transparency, and the need for genuine connection as he sought to make sense of the mysteries that had marked his journey of love.

PHINDILE'S MYSTERIOUS disappearance left Sibusiso with profound lessons about the art of letting go and the importance of finding closure in matters of the heart.

1. **The Challenge of Letting Go:** Phindile's sudden departure presented Sibusiso with the challenge of letting go of a relationship clouded by mystery and uncertainty. He realized that sometimes, despite his desire for answers, letting go was the healthiest choice for his own well-being.

2. **The Quest for Closure:** Sibusiso understood the value of seeking closure in relationships. Phindile's disappearance highlighted the need to understand and resolve unresolved questions and emotions. He learned that finding closure allowed him to move forward with a sense of peace and acceptance.

3. **The Acceptance of Unanswered Questions:** Sibusiso came to terms with the reality that not all questions would have answers. Phindile's enigmatic nature meant that some mysteries might never be solved, and he learned to accept that ambiguity as a part of life.

4. **The Importance of Self-Care:** In the wake of Phindile's disappearance, Sibusiso embraced the importance of self-care and healing. He recognized that taking time to grieve and process the loss of a relationship, even one marked by mystery, was essential for his emotional well-being.

5. **The Journey to Finding Authentic Love:** Phindile's departure renewed Sibusiso's commitment to finding authentic love. He understood that love should be built on trust, transparency, and genuine connection, and he resolved to seek a relationship that offered these qualities.

As Sibusiso continued his quest for love, these lessons about letting go and finding closure would guide him in his pursuit of meaningful and transparent relationships. He had learned that love was not always a puzzle to be solved but sometimes a journey of self-discovery and acceptance, where closure marked the path to a new beginning.

Chapter 15: Nqobile's Redemption

Nqobile, a woman with a heart filled with compassion and a genuine desire to make amends, entered Sibusiso's life like a beacon of hope. Their love story continued to unfold against the backdrop of Durban's healing waves, where the city's gentle rhythm mirrored their journey toward forgiveness and redemption.

Nqobile's warmth and her unwavering commitment to making things right drew Sibusiso in from the very beginning. Their love was a story of redemption, marked by forgiveness, growth, and dreams of a future built on a foundation of understanding and compassion.

Nqobile carried with her a past marked by mistakes and regrets, including her own experiences with infidelity and betrayal. Yet, she was determined to learn from her past and create a better future, not only for herself but also for the love she shared with Sibusiso.

As they navigated the complexities of their relationship, Nqobile's love became a source of healing for Sibusiso's wounded heart. Her commitment to transparency, honesty, and genuine connection helped him mend the scars left by his previous experiences of betrayal and heartbreak.

With Nqobile, Sibusiso learned the transformative power of love that was rooted in empathy and redemption. He realized that sometimes, love had the capacity to heal old wounds, and that growth and change were possible, even after the pain of betrayal.

This chapter in Sibusiso's journey would lead him toward a deeper understanding of the capacity for redemption within himself and others. It would leave him with lessons about the resilience of the human spirit and the enduring hope for love that was built on trust, forgiveness, and the possibility of renewal.

NQOBILE'S LOVE AND their journey of healing and growth taught Sibusiso about the profound transformative power of love in one's life.

1. **The Healing Power of Love:** Through Nqobile's love and her commitment to making amends, Sibusiso experienced firsthand the healing power of love. He realized that love had the capacity to mend even the deepest wounds, offering solace and a path toward renewal.

2. **The Possibility of Redemption:** Nqobile's story of redemption demonstrated that people could learn from their mistakes and grow as individuals. Sibusiso understood that love had the power to inspire change and encourage individuals to become their better selves.

3. **The Importance of Empathy:** Nqobile's empathy and understanding were invaluable in their journey. Sibusiso learned that empathy was a powerful tool in building connections and fostering forgiveness. It allowed him to see beyond the mistakes of the past and embrace the potential for positive change.

4. **The Value of Transparency:** Transparency became a cornerstone of their relationship with Nqobile. Sibusiso recognized that open and honest communication was vital for trust and healing. It allowed him to share his own vulnerabilities and fears, deepening their connection.

5. **The Hope for Renewed Love:** Through Nqobile, Sibusiso discovered that love could be renewed and strengthened even after experiencing betrayal and heartbreak. He realized that a love grounded in forgiveness and compassion had the potential to be even more profound and enduring.

As Sibusiso continued his quest for love, these lessons about the transformative nature of love would guide him in his pursuit of meaningful and genuine relationships. He had learned that love had he power to heal, inspire growth, and lead individuals toward a future marked by hope and renewal.

Chapter 16: Noluthando's Unconditional Love

Noluthando, a woman with a heart overflowing with unwavering love and boundless kindness, entered Sibusiso's life like a beacon of serenity. Their love story unfolded against the backdrop of Durban's tranquil beaches, where the ocean's gentle waves mirrored the calm and understanding that defined their connection.

Noluthando's love was marked by its unconditional nature, a love that knew no judgment or conditions. From the moment she entered Sibusiso's life, she embraced him with a warmth that made him feel valued and accepted, scars and all.

With Noluthando, Sibusiso experienced a love that was pure, patient, and profoundly healing. Her capacity for forgiveness and her open-hearted approach allowed him to let go of the burdens of his past and step into the light of acceptance and love.

Through her unwavering support and her belief in his capacity for love and happiness, Noluthando prepared Sibusiso for the arrival of his soulmate, Nokulunga Cele. With Noluthando, he learned the invaluable lessons of self-acceptance, the beauty of unconditional love, and the importance of being ready to embrace the kindred spirit meant for him.

As Sibusiso's journey came full circle, he recognized that Noluthando's love had been a crucial stepping stone on his path to finding his true soulmate. She had shown him the transformative power of love that accepted him for who he was, setting the stage for the profound connection he would ultimately discover with Nokulunga.

This final chapter in Sibusiso's journey would leave him with lessons about the enduring impact of unconditional love and the profound sense of readiness that comes when one's heart is truly open to the love of a lifetime.

NOLUTHANDO'S UNWAVERING and unconditional love taught Sibusiso a profound lesson about the beauty and transformative power of love that knows no conditions.

1. **The Beauty of Acceptance:** Through Noluthando's love, Sibusiso experienced the beauty of being accepted for who he truly was, flaws and all. He realized that love that imposed no conditions allowed individuals to embrace their authentic selves without fear of judgment.

2. **The Healing Nature of Unconditional Love:** Noluthando's love had a healing quality. It helped Sibusiso release the wounds and insecurities from his past, allowing him to step into the present with a sense of wholeness and self-acceptance.

3. **The Capacity for Forgiveness:** Noluthando's unconditional love showcased the capacity for forgiveness and compassion that love could embody. Sibusiso learned that love could transcend past mistakes and offer a chance for redemption and growth.

4. **The Power of Patience:** Noluthando's patient love taught Sibusiso about the value of patience in relationships. He understood that love didn't rush or demand immediate change but allowed individuals to evolve and grow at their own pace.

5. **The Readiness to Soulmate love:** Through Noluthando's love, Sibusiso became emotionally ready to embrace the love of his soulmate, Nokulunga Cele. He realized that the beauty of unconditional love was that it prepared the heart to welcome a profound and enduring connection.

As Sibusiso's journey came to a close, he carried with him the profound understanding that unconditional love was a gift that could transform lives, heal wounds, and ultimately prepare the heart for the love it had been destined to find. He had learned that love, at its core, was a force that had the power to make individuals better versions of themselves and to create a future marked by hope, acceptance, and the beauty of boundless love.

Through these tumultuous relationships and their various forms of cheating, Sibusiso's character evolves, and he gains valuable insights into the complexities of love and human nature. These experiences shape him, paving the way for his destined encounter with Nokulunga Cele.

Chapter 17: Nokulunga Cele

Nokulunga Cele, a woman shrouded in an aura of mystery and intrigue, stepped into Sibusiso's life like a whisper of fate. Their encounter unfolded against the backdrop of Durban's enchanting evenings, where the city's lights seemed to illuminate the path leading them to each other.

From the moment he first laid eyes on her, Sibusiso sensed that Nokulunga was different. She possessed an air of quiet confidence, her eyes held a depth of wisdom, and her smile hinted at secrets yet to be revealed.

Their initial interactions were marked by a sense of familiarity, as if they had known each other in another lifetime. Nokulunga was a woman of few words, yet her presence spoke volumes. She carried with her an air of mystery that left Sibusiso both intrigued and captivated.

As they began to share stories and dreams, Sibusiso discovered that Nokulunga had a unique perspective on life, love, and the world. Her wisdom and insights resonated deeply with him, and he felt drawn to unravel the enigma that was Nokulunga Cele.

In Nokulunga, Sibusiso sensed the possibility of a profound and enduring connection, one that transcended the trials and tribulations of his past relationships. Their journey together was destined to be marked by discovery, understanding, and the promise of a love that felt fated to be.

This chapter in Sibusiso's journey marked the beginning of a new and captivating love story, one in which he would explore the depths of his connection with Nokulunga Cele and discover the secrets hidden within their intertwined destinies.

THEIR INITIAL ENCOUNTERS were marked by a sense of serendipity, as if the universe had conspired to bring Sibusiso and Nokulunga Cele together. It was a warm evening in Durban, and Sibusiso found himself at a local art gallery, drawn by his love for creativity and culture.

As he moved through the gallery, admiring the vibrant paintings and sculptures, his attention was captured by a woman who seemed to be immersed in the art just like him. She stood before a canvas, her eyes fixed on the intricate details of a painting that seemed to speak to her soul.

Sibusiso couldn't resist the urge to strike up a conversation. He approached her with a gentle smile, "That painting has a way of drawing you in, doesn't it?"

Nokulunga turned to him, her eyes reflecting a mixture of surprise and appreciation for the shared connection. "Yes, it does," she replied softly, "It's as if the artist has captured a piece of their own soul in it."

Their conversation flowed effortlessly from there, as if they had known each other for a lifetime. They shared their thoughts on art, life, and the mysteries of the universe. Nokulunga's insights resonated deeply with Sibusiso, and he found himself hanging onto her every word.

After that initial encounter, they continued to meet at various art events, cafes, and even by the ocean, where they would sit in companionable silence, gazing at the waves as if contemplating the secrets of the universe.

Nokulunga's presence in Sibusiso's life was like a missing piece of a puzzle falling into place. Their connection was not just based on shared interests but on a profound sense of understanding and acceptance. It was as if they had been searching for each other across lifetimes, and now, fate had finally brought them together.

In Nokulunga Cele, Sibusiso found not only a kindred spirit but also a source of inspiration and hope. Their connection was marked by a sense of destiny, as if their love story had been written in the stars, waiting to be discovered one serendipitous encounter at a time.

Chapter 18: Sibusiso's Transformation

Sibusiso's journey through the tumultuous terrain of love, filled with experiences of cheating, had transformed him in profound ways. Each betrayal, heartbreak, and lesson learned had left an indelible mark on his character and outlook on life.

1. **Heightened Awareness:** Sibusiso's experiences with cheating had sharpened his awareness of the complexities of human relationships. He had become attuned to the subtle signs of deceit and infidelity, making him more perceptive in his future interactions.

2. **Resilience:** The pain of betrayal and heartbreak had tested Sibusiso's resilience. He had discovered an inner strength that allowed him to bounce back from adversity, no matter how deep the wounds. His ability to endure and grow stronger had become a hallmark of his character.

3. **Empathy:** Sibusiso's own experiences had made him more empathetic toward others facing similar challenges. He understood the emotional toll of betrayal and sought to offer support and understanding to those in need.

4. **Value of Communication:** The breakdown of trust in his previous relationships had underscored the importance of open and honest communication. Sibusiso had become a proponent of transparent conversations as the foundation of healthy relationships.

5. **Forgiveness:** Sibusiso had learned the art of forgiveness. He understood that holding onto anger and resentment only burdened his own heart. Forgiving those who had betrayed him had freed him from the weight of the past.

6. **Desire for Authenticity:** His experiences had instilled in him a deep desire for authenticity in love. Sibusiso sought genuine connections built on trust and transparency, valuing quality over quantity in his relationships.

7. **Readiness for Soulmate Love:** Through his journey, Sibusiso had reached a state of emotional readiness for the kind of love he had always longed for. His transformation had prepared him to fully embrace the love of his soulmate, Nokulunga Cele, with an open heart.

Sibusiso had evolved from a young man filled with idealistic notions of love to a wiser and more resilient individual. His experiences had shaped him into someone who understood that love, though often challenging, was a journey of self-discovery, growth, and the possibility of finding a love that was truly meant to be.

As Sibusiso reflected on his personal growth and newfound wisdom about relationships, he realized just how far he had come on his journey of love. His experiences with cheating had imparted valuable lessons that had transformed him into a more mature and insightful individual.

1. **Embracing Vulnerability:** Sibusiso had learned that vulnerability was not a weakness but a strength. He understood that opening up and sharing his feelings with a partner was essential for building trust and intimacy.

2. **Prioritizing Self-Care:** His journey had taught him the importance of self-care and self-love. Sibusiso recognized that taking care of his own emotional well-being was crucial to forming healthy relationships.

3. **Valuing Trust Above All:** Trust had become the cornerstone of his approach to relationships. Sibusiso knew that without trust, love was fragile, and he made it a point to cultivate trust in his connections.

4. **Embracing Imperfections:** He had come to accept that no one was perfect, including himself. Sibusiso had learned to embrace his own imperfections and those of his partners, understanding that love was about loving the whole person.

5. **Setting Boundaries:** Sibusiso had become adept at setting boundaries in his relationships. He understood that healthy boundaries were essential for maintaining respect and harmony.

6. **Choosing Quality Over Quantity:** He had shifted his focus from pursuing many relationships to seeking quality connections. Sibusiso valued depth and authenticity over superficial interactions.

7. **Cultivating Patience:** His experiences had taught him the virtue of patience in love. Sibusiso had learned that genuine connections took time to develop, and he was willing to invest that time.

8. **The Power of Forgiveness:** Forgiveness had become one of his guiding principles. Sibusiso had realized that holding onto grudges only hindered his own growth and ability to love fully.

9. **Seeking Mutual Growth:** He now believed that the best relationships were those where both partners supported each other's growth and development.

10. **Ready for Soulmate Love:** Sibusiso's transformation had readied him for the love he had always sought. He was open to the idea that his soulmate, Nokulunga Cele, might be the culmination of his journey—a love that was profound, enduring, and destined to be.

Sibusiso's personal growth and wisdom about relationships had not only made him a better partner but also a more fulfilled individual. He understood that the journey of love was as much about self-discovery as it was about finding a soulmate, and he was ready to embrace whatever lay ahead with an open heart and newfound wisdom.

Chapter 19: The Journey to Finding True Love

Sibusiso and Nokulunga's relationship unfolded like a beautifully composed symphony, each note resonating with the harmony of their souls. Their love story was marked by a profound evolution, demonstrating the depths of connection that could be achieved when two kindred spirits came together.

1. **The Foundation of Friendship:** Their relationship began with a strong foundation of friendship. Sibusiso and Nokulunga spent hours talking, sharing their dreams, and exploring the world together. They cherished each other's company, and their laughter filled the spaces between their conversations.

2. **Trust and Transparency:** Sibusiso and Nokulunga had learned the importance of trust and transparency in their past experiences. They were open and honest with each other, sharing their fears, insecurities, and dreams without reservation. Trust blossomed like a delicate flower in the garden of their love.

3. **Shared Values and Goals:** They discovered that their values and life goals aligned seamlessly. Both were driven by a passion for personal growth, a love for art and culture, and a desire to create a meaningful impact on the world. Their shared vision for the future strengthened their bond.

4. **Support and Encouragement:** Sibusiso and Nokulunga were each other's greatest supporters. They cheered on each other's achievements and provided comfort during moments of doubt. Their love was a safe haven where they could seek refuge from life's challenges.

5. Growth and Self-Discovery: Their relationship became a catalyst for personal growth and self-discovery. Sibusiso and Nokulunga encouraged each other to pursue their passions and dreams, nurturing an environment where they could flourish as individuals.

6. Adventure and Exploration: Their love story was an adventure in itself. They embarked on journeys together, exploring new places, cultures, and experiences. Each adventure strengthened their connection and created cherished memories.

7. Unconditional Love: Sibusiso and Nokulunga's love was marked by its unconditional nature. They accepted each other's flaws and imperfections, understanding that it was these very qualities that made them unique and lovable.

8. Preparation for Forever: Their journey together felt like the preparation for forever. Sibusiso knew in his heart that Nokulunga was the missing piece he had been searching for, and Nokulunga felt the same. Their love was profound, enduring, and destined to stand the test of time.

Sibusiso and Nokulunga's relationship was a testament to the transformative power of love. It was a love that had evolved from the lessons of the past, blossomed into a beautiful present, and held the promise of an even brighter future. Together, they had found the true love they had both been seeking—a love that felt destined, enduring, and meant to be.

1. Past Baggage: Both Sibusiso and Nokulunga carried the scars of past relationships, marked by infidelity and betrayal. Initially, these scars caused moments of insecurity and doubt. However, they openly discussed their past experiences, providing support and understanding to each other as they worked through their emotional baggage.

2. Balancing Personal Aspirations: Sibusiso was passionate about his career, and Nokulunga was equally driven in her pursuits. Balancing heir personal aspirations with their relationship required careful planning and compromise. They learned to prioritize their dreams while nurturing their love.

3. **Family Expectations:** Cultural and familial expectations occasionally created tension. Sibusiso and Nokulunga came from different backgrounds with unique customs and traditions. Through respectful conversations and a willingness to learn from each other, they found ways to bridge the gap between their families and their relationship.

4. **Distance:** There were times when distance separated them due to work or personal commitments. Instead of letting it strain their connection, they used this time apart as an opportunity to strengthen their emotional bond, maintaining open communication through calls, messages, and video chats.

5. **Miscommunications:** Like any couple, they had moments of miscommunication and misunderstandings. Yet, they had learned from their past experiences the importance of clear and honest communication. They patiently discussed their concerns and actively listened to each other's perspectives, resolving issues with empathy.

6. **External Pressures:** The pressures of societal expectations and external opinions occasionally tested their love. Sibusiso and Nokulunga stayed united against these pressures, reinforcing their belief in their love and the importance of following their hearts.

7. **Personal Growth:** As they continued to grow individually, they occasionally experienced moments of self-discovery and change. Instead of fearing these transformations, they celebrated each other's personal growth, recognizing that it was a natural part of their journey together.

8. **Life's Uncertainties:** Life brought its own uncertainties and challenges, from health issues to unforeseen obstacles. Sibusiso and Nokulunga faced these challenges with resilience and unwavering support, reminding each other that they were stronger together.

Through these challenges, Sibusiso and Nokulunga's love only grew stronger. Their commitment to each other and their willingness to face adversity together demonstrated the depth of their connection. Their love story was a testament to the idea that true love wasn't immune to challenges but rather thrived in their presence, becoming a source of strength and resilience.

Chapter 20: The Revelation

The gentle breeze off the Durban coast carried a sense of serenity as Sibusiso and Nokulunga strolled along the beach, hand in hand. The moonlight danced on the waves, casting a silvery glow over their path, seemingly in sync with the harmony of their love.

As they walked, the conversation turned to their shared dreams and aspirations. Sibusiso, with a heart full of hope, spoke about his desire to start a family and raise children in a loving home. Nokulunga listened attentively, her eyes reflecting the depth of her emotions.

Then, with a mixture of vulnerability and hesitation, Nokulunga finally shared her revelation, a twist that would test the strength of their love in ways they could not have anticipated.

"I need to tell you something," Nokulunga began, her voice gentle but filled with a profound truth. "I've always dreamed of having a family too, but there's something you should know."

Sibusiso looked into her eyes, his heart filled with curiosity and love. "What is it, my love? You can tell me anything."

Nokulunga took a deep breath. "I have a child—a beautiful daughter named Zinhle. She's the light of my life, and I've raised her as a single mother."

Sibusiso was taken aback, not by the revelation itself but by the depth of Nokulunga's courage in sharing it. He took a moment to absorb the information, realizing that this twist in their love story was an opportunity to strengthen their bond.

Instead of reacting with shock or judgment, Sibusiso embraced Nokulunga, holding her close. "Thank you for sharing this with me," he whispered. "Your honesty means the world to me, and I love you even more for it."

Their love, which had weathered storms and faced challenges head-on, was now put to the test once again. This revelation would require them to navigate the complexities of blending their lives and raising a child together. It was a surprise that neither had anticipated, but their unwavering commitment to each other would guide them through this new chapter of their love story, one that held the promise of even greater depth and resilience.

Chapter 21: The Resolution

In the aftermath of Nokulunga's revelation about her daughter, Zinhle, Sibusiso and Nokulunga faced the challenges and joys of blending their lives into a beautiful tapestry of love and family. Their journey together was a testament to the strength of their bond and their commitment to making their love story work, regardless of the obstacles in their path.

Over time, Sibusiso developed a loving relationship with Zinhle, treating her as if she were his own daughter. The little girl's laughter filled their home, and her presence brought a newfound sense of completeness to their lives.

As a family, they faced the world with love, resilience, and the determination to create a nurturing and harmonious environment for Zinhle to grow. They overcame the complexities of blending their lives, finding strength in their love for each other and for the young girl who had become the heart of their family.

Their relationship continued to evolve, marked by moments of laughter, shared dreams, and the deepening of their emotional connection. Sibusiso and Nokulunga's love story was not without challenges, but it was a testament to their unwavering commitment to each other and their shared vision of a life filled with love, understanding, and support.

In the end, their love story found a resolution that was not only satisfying but also deeply enriching. It was a love story that had evolved, grown, and thrived in the face of adversity. Sibusiso, Nokulunga, and Zinhle became a family bound by love, united by the shared dream of a future filled with warmth, laughter, and the enduring embrace of a love that was truly meant to be.

Epilogue

Years passed, and the love between Sibusiso, Nokulunga, and Zinhle continued to flourish. Their family was a testament to the power of love, resilience, and the beauty of unexpected twists in life's journey.

Sibusiso and Nokulunga's love had deepened with time, becoming a foundation of strength for their family. They had faced life's challenges together, supporting each other in their individual pursuits and nurturing their shared dreams.

Zinhle, the beautiful child who had once been the subject of a surprising revelation, had grown into a remarkable young woman. She carried the wisdom of her parents' love with her, understanding the importance of trust, honesty, and the capacity for love to heal and transform.

Their home was filled with laughter, shared meals, and the comforting warmth of a love that had weathered storms and emerged stronger. They had created a haven where love was the guiding force, where challenges were met with grace, and where every day was a reminder of the beauty of family.

Sibusiso, Nokulunga, and Zinhle's love story was one of resilience, personal growth, and the triumph of love over adversity. It was a story that showcased the power of the human spirit to overcome challenges and the enduring strength of a love that was destined to be.

And as they gazed out at the Durban coast, where their journey had begun, they knew that their love story was a testament to the idea that true love, once found, could endure, evolve, and create a future filled with hope, laughter, and the boundless beauty of family.

Throughout the story, we covered various subjects and themes, including:

1. Love and Relationships: The central theme of the story revolved around Sibusiso's journey to find true love, exploring the complexities, challenges, and transformative power of romantic relationships.

2. Cheating and Betrayal: The story delved into the painful experiences of cheating and betrayal that Sibusiso encountered in his previous relationships, highlighting the emotional toll they took and the lessons learned.

3. Personal Growth: Sibusiso's character development was a significant focus, as he evolved from a young man seeking love to a mature individual who had learned valuable life lessons about trust, communication, and self-acceptance.

4. Resilience and Forgiveness: The story emphasized the resilience of the human spirit and the capacity for forgiveness, showing how characters faced adversity and grew stronger through forgiveness and empathy.

5. Family and Blending Lives: The story explored the challenges and joys of blending lives and families, with the revelation of Nokulunga's daughter, Zinhle, and how Sibusiso and Nokulunga navigated the complexities of raising a child together.

6. Communication and Trust: The importance of open and honest communication, as well as the significance of trust in building and maintaining healthy relationships, was a recurring theme.

7. Unconditional Love: The story portrayed the beauty of unconditional love, emphasizing the acceptance of each other's imperfections and the depth of love that transcends conditions and expectations.

8. Personal and Family Values: The characters' shared values and life goals played a crucial role in their relationship, highlighting the significance of aligning one's values with a partner's.

9. Growth and Transformation: Sibusiso's personal growth and transformation as he learned from past experiences and became a more resilient and empathetic individual were central to the narrative.

10. The Power of Fate and Serendipity: The story often touched on the idea of fate and serendipitous encounters, suggesting that some connections are destined to happen.

These themes and subjects collectively created a rich and engaging narrative that followed the characters through their ups and downs, ultimately leading to a satisfying resolution.

Don't miss out!

Visit the website below and you can sign up to receive emails whenever Sibusiso Anthon Mkhwanazi publishes a new book. There's no charge and no obligation.

https://books2read.com/r/B-A-QNVAB-MJFPC

BOOKS 2 READ

Connecting independent readers to independent writers.

Did you love *Cheating hearts to true love*? Then you should read *Million-Dollar Decade*[1] by Sibusiso Anthon Mkhwanazi!

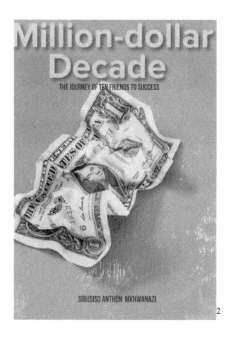

[2]

Book Description: Million-Dollar Decade: The Journey of Ten Friends

In the heart of Daveyton, a small town in Gauteng, South Africa, ten friends embarked on a remarkable journey that would change their lives and the world of art forever. "Million-Dollar Decade" is the captivating tale of their extraordinary odyssey from humble beginnings to becoming millionaires, all while staying true to their values and fostering the enduring power of friendship.

Within these pages, you'll uncover the secrets of their success, forged through a shared passion for art, a commitment to local talent, and a vision that transcended borders. Their story unfolds as they build the

Daveyton Artistry Hub, a platform that not only elevates artists but also revitalizes their community and inspires a global audience.

"Million-Dollar Decade" takes you on a journey of creativity, resilience, and transformation. It's a story that underscores the importance of staying true to your values, embracing diversity, and giving back to the community. Through their trials and triumphs, these ten friends become philanthropists, changemakers, and champions of creativity, leaving a legacy that transcends financial wealth.

Their tale of empowerment, artistic innovation, and the enduring bonds of friendship will inspire aspiring entrepreneurs, artists, and anyone who believes in the transformative power of following their dreams. "Million-Dollar Decade" invites you to join the journey, celebrate local talent, and discover the profound impact of friendship on the path to success.

Prepare to be inspired, uplifted, and reminded that with unwavering commitment, dreams can become reality, and the journey itself can be as rewarding as the destination.

Read more at Vukuphande.co.za.

Milton Keynes UK
Ingram Content Group UK Ltd.
UKHW020944221123
433051UK00020B/959